DIFFERENTIATING TEXTBOOKS

DIFFERENTIATING TEXTBOOKS

Strategies to Improve Student Comprehension & Motivation

Char Forsten, Jim Grant, and Betty Hollas

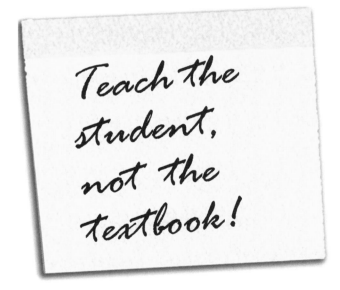

Teach the student, not the textbook!

Crystal Springs
SDE BOOKS
a division of Staff Development for Educators
Peterborough, New Hampshire
www.SDE.com/crystalsprings

Published by Crystal Springs Books
A division of Staff Development for Educators (SDE)
10 Sharon Road
P.O. Box 500
Peterborough, NH 03458
1-800-321-0401
www.SDE.com/crystalsprings

Printed in the United States of America
13 12 11   6 7 8 9

ISBN: 978-1-884548-48-2

Library of Congress Cataloging-in-Publication Data

Forsten, Char, 1948-
  Differentiating textbooks : strategies to improve student
comprehension & motivation / by Char Forsten, Jim Grant, and Betty Hollas.
      p. cm.
Includes bibliographical references and index.
  ISBN 978-1-884548-48-2
  1. Individualized reading instruction. 2. Content area reading. 3.
Textbooks—Readability. 4. Reading comprehension. I. Grant, Jim, 1942-
II. Hollas, Betty, 1948- III. Title.
  LB1050.38.F69 2003
  372.41'7—dc21
                          2003000272

Editor: Sandra Taylor
Art Director, Designer, and Production Coordinator: S. Dunholter
Publishing Projects Coordinator: Deborah Fredericks
Illustrator: Carl Witham

Some strategies in this book have been adapted from material listed in the Resources section. We welcome information to correct any oversights in subsequent editions. Also, the authors would appreciate other suggestions for future editions of this book.

Dedication

To Dr. Jean Ciborowski, whose seminal work, *Textbooks and the Students Who Can't Read Them*, is the "Rosetta stone" that has unlocked the mystery of why so many students struggle with textbook learning. Her courage to present the unabashed truth inspired us to create this book.

Table of Contents

Acknowledgments IX
Introduction XI

Chapter 1:
Ways to Create Random Groupings   13

Equivalent Decimals, Percents, and Fractions . 14
Popsicle Sticks for Grouping 15
Creating Groups of Four with Attribute Cards 16
Pairing Up for Learning 18
Clock Partners 19
Circle of Three 20
Card Games for Grouping 21

Chapter 2:
Selecting and Adapting Textbooks   23

Laminated Chapter Books 24
Smaller Is Better 25
Substitute Headings and Subheadings 26
Eliminate Unnecessary Information 27
Circle and Box Math Problems 28
Large-Print Textbooks.................................. 29
Textbook Adaptation Plan 30

Chapter 3:
Before-Reading Strategies   31

Concept Map: A New Version of KWL 32
Compacting Textbook Chapters 34
Pros, Cons, and "What I Wonder" 36
Guess the Word 37
Vocabulary Index Cards 38
Taped Vocabulary Words 39

Talking Flash Cards 40
Online Vocabulary Help 41
List-Group-Label 42
Anticipation Guide 43
Timed Responses 44
Cloze Activity 45
Greet and Go 46
Word Toss 47
Thinking Aloud: A Fix-Up Strategy 48
Overhead Textbook Visuals 49
Clear Up Math Visuals 50
Estimating Math Answers 51
Pointer/Signal Words and Text Structure 52
R.S.V.P. 53
Highlighting Text 54

Chapter 4:
During-Reading Strategies   55

Keep-Your-Place Reading Tool 56
Colored Overlays to Bring Print into Focus 57
Post-It Notes and Codes 58
Using a Focus Frame 60
Active Bookmarks 61
Eliminate Transferring Time and Copying
   Errors 62
Drawing the Words 63
Recorded Textbooks 64
Noise-Suppressing Headphones for
   Concentrating.. 65
Power Thinking 66
Content Puzzles 68
Note Taking with Graphic Organizers 69

Textbook Talk-back Notes 70
Read-Pair-Share 71
Three-Step Interview 72
Personal Learning Timelines 73
Math Word Problem Graphic Organizer 74
Mind-Mapping for Understanding 75
Hearing the Text: Onomatopoeia 76

Chapter 5:
After-Reading Strategies   *77*

Inside/Outside Review Circles 78
Give All or Part of the Answer 79
Crossword Puzzles: Standard, Backward, and
     In-between 80
Information Grid: Organizing, Categorizing,
     and Analyzing 81
Leveling Questions 82
Potluck Reading 84
Transforming Information in the Text 85
R.A.F.T. 86
Textbook Pictionary 87
Three Facts and a Fib 88
Taped Responses 89
Text Souvenirs 90
Exit Cards to Summarize 91
Answer by the Number 92
Pieces of Eight 93
Four Corners Voting 94
Match-the-Meaning Card Game 95
R.E.A.D.S. 96
Textbook Look-back 98
Writing Summaries 99
And That's the Rest of the Story 100

Appendix (Reproducibles)   *101*

Resources   *143*

Reference Works and Research 144
Products, Supplies, and Adaptive Services 149
Educational Organizations 151
Helpful Web Sites 152

Index   *153*

Acknowledgments

Special thanks to:

Sandy Taylor, our extraordinary editor—whose ability to blend the writing of three authors into one voice is truly a gift.

Soosen Dunholter, our world-class designer—whose keen eye always brings our words to life.

Deb Fredericks, project coordinator—the driving force that kept this project on schedule.

Lorraine Walker, vice president of Staff Development for Educators and Crystal Springs Books—the champion of this book.

Cathie Runyon, administrative assistant—who tirelessly verified details and research to bring this book to press.

Dick Dunning, principal, South Meadow School—an endless source of great ideas.

Harriet Tyson-Bernstein, author, *America's Textbook Fiasco*—whose writing provided much-needed inspiration.

Caspar Grathwohl, editor, Oxford University Press, USA—who had the courage to publish *A History of US*, a student-centered textbook series.

Introduction

Differentiating textbooks—just what does that mean? Basically, it is modifying or adapting textbooks in ways that make them easier for students to read and comprehend, and then to retain what they have read. Instead of teaching the textbook, the emphasis is on teaching the student.

You, as a teacher, know full well that students vary greatly in the ways that they learn, so textbook accommodations and adaptations should be driven by what works best for the individual. The strategies we have included here are aimed at all students—not just struggling learners, although identified special needs and 504 students (those not identified as having special needs but who do require accommodations of some kind) will benefit greatly from them as well.

Expository vs. Narrative Text

Young students up through third grade are familiar with the format and structure of narrative text, or story form. They know by heart its characteristics and predictable nature—that it has a beginning, a middle, and an end; a setting (or settings); characters; plot; events; and resolutions. Starting around the fourth grade, students are introduced to expository text, yet many are unprepared for this major shift in focus, involving question and answer, compare and contrast, listing, cause and effect, and problem and solution. Even those who understand or can quickly grasp these concepts may still struggle with expository text—and for many reasons.

First, textbooks tend to be written in a formulaic style that is choppy, uninspired, and disjointed. In addition, main ideas often are implied and embedded in the text. The chapter headings and subheadings may be vague or ambiguous, and the topics superficial and lacking in substance. Written in the "mentioning mode," without voice or style, many textbooks often try to do too much and rely on "compression writing" to cover as many topics as possible. On the whole, such textbooks can make reading comprehension difficult for the average student and nearly impossible for the struggling reader. But even textbooks of the poorest quality can be used effectively by employing the strategies and activities described in this book.

A great deal can be done to help students comprehend expository text, but one of the most important things to remember is that many of the principles employed in teaching narrative fictional literature can and should be applied to teaching content-area material. In short, reading nonfiction can be as engaging and appealing as reading fiction or narrative text.

Modeling, Guided Practice, and Independence

The main goal of this book is to create independent learners who apply the techniques used here to other classes, across the curriculum, during their educational years, and continue to use them throughout their lives. To achieve this, start first by modeling each strategy for your students, doing it by yourself and "thinking aloud" as you go through the steps. Begin with something that is familiar so your students can quickly reach a comfort level with an activity before attempting it with more difficult material.

Next, provide plenty of opportunities for guided practice. Occasionally, you may have to reinforce strategies repeatedly for some students. Others in the class will be able to make them their own, use them independently, and eventually learn how to monitor their own comprehension.

Random Groupings

When implementing the strategies we offer here, you will sometimes want your students to collaborate and work together. To save you valuable time, we have devoted an entire chapter to quick, easy, and efficient ways to get your students organized into pairs or small groups. Some of these techniques even teach or reinforce skills as your students locate their partners.

Before, During, and After

Differentiating Textbooks provides highly effective before-, during-, and after-reading strategies that help students understand the text. Whatever their reading level or ability to comprehend expository text might be, it is up to you to make the textbook material accessible and meaningful, and we have included a number of ways to help you do this. Remember, though, that not every student will relate to each and every strategy.

To increase your chances of reaching struggling learners, you might want to use a combination of strategies for one task. Some strategies adapt to or work better in different curricular areas than others, so experiment to see what best fits your classroom needs. As with differentiated instruction, you will soon discover that differentiating textbooks is "just part of good teaching."

Ways to Create Random Groupings

There are three basic types of grouping arrangements for getting students together when you want them to work in collaboration with others. These are:

- **Student selected**—This is a quick way to get groups formed, but students are more likely to always join the same friends and thereby miss the opportunity to work with other, less familiar classmates.

- **Teacher determined**—When you decide on the learning objectives, you can group students according to their needs, skills attainment, and interests. Although somewhat permanent, these are flexible in nature. Students gain more independence when grouped according to varying strengths because they are able to help and support each other. When grouping for instructional purposes, such as for mini-lessons, you can arrange groups by similarity of needs. Other groupings can be done for community building and management, which can help with behavioral issues and promote friendship.

- **Randomly selected**—This chapter describes a variety of ways to form randomly selected groups quickly when you want your students to work in pairs or small, heterogeneous groups. Having these techniques at hand will save you valuable time, prevent the same students from repeatedly working together, and enable you to teach or reinforce skills at the same time that students seek out their grouping partner(s).

Occasionally, you will find that there will be one or more students left without a group to join. For instance, if your grouping method calls for three students to work together but there is an extra student, you might have him or her partner with one of the students in an already-formed group and work together as one. Or, if you have grouped into threes and one of your groups has only two students, you might join that group as the third member, assuming that you don't need to monitor what is happening in the classroom. These are just a couple of ways to resolve this situation, so use your imagination and come up with ideas that work best for you and for your students' grade level.

Equivalent Decimals, Percents, and Fractions

Explanation:

There are times when a group of three students is needed for an activity. This grouping technique reinforces decimals, fractions, and percents at the same time that it gets students together in threes.

Materials:

- Index cards or Math Equivalents Cards reproducible (see pages 102-103)

Directions:

1. Write decimals, fractions, and percents of like value on index cards, one per card, or duplicate the reproducible math cards.

2. When it is time to group students, give each one a card that has either a decimal, a fraction, or a percent written on it.

3. Have students move around the room to find their equivalent partners (for example: ¼, .25, 25%).

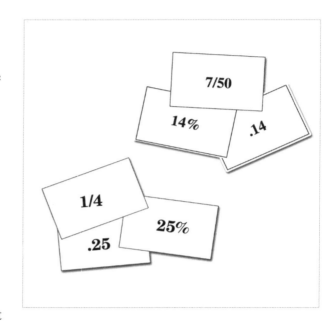

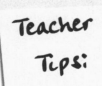

Teacher Tips:

1. Use improper fractions and their counterparts.
2. If possible, laminate the cards for long-term use.

Popsicle Sticks for Grouping

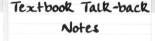

Explanation:

This technique provides an easy way to group your students randomly, using simple materials and minimal preparation time.

Materials:

- Popsicle or craft sticks (as many as there are students in class)

Directions:

1. Using Popsicle, regular size, or wide craft sticks, write each student's name on one stick.

2. Store the sticks in an envelope or a can for future use.

3. When it is time to create groups, randomly gather the sticks in bunches of three, four, five, etc., depending on the desired group size.

4. Call out the students' names for each group and assign the activity they are to work on together.

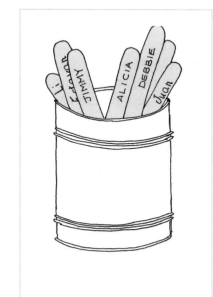

Teacher Tips:

1. A variation on this theme involves colored craft sticks, which are available at most craft and teacher stores. You can use them to group students in either a preplanned or random fashion. Buy packages containing four or five different colors of sticks.

2. To preplan your groups, you first need to decide which students you want to work together and write each student's name for the same group on the same color of stick. Pass out the sticks and instruct your students to find others who share the same color. When assigned by color, students always work with the same group.

3. To group randomly, simply ignore the colors and follow the same procedure described in the directions above.

Textbook Talk-back Notes

Creating Groups of Four with Attribute Cards

Explanation:

This technique uses attributes and provides five different ways to put students together quickly and differently throughout the year. When preparing for an activity that requires grouping, pass out the attribute cards. Identify a grouping attribute and have students get into groups accordingly. For example, one day you might instruct students to form groups of the same color; another time, you might tell them to group by the same shape or by the same sticker, part of speech, or number.

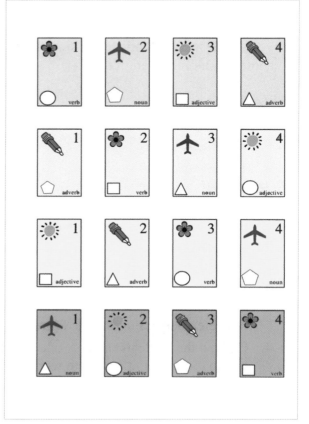

Materials:

- 3x5-inch index cards of four different colors or Attribute Cards reproducible (see page 104)
- Stickers of four different types (flowers or insects work well)

Directions:

1. If using index cards, lay them out in a 4x4 grid so that each color forms a row. In the upper right-hand corner of each card, number each color set from one to four.

2. For the remaining attributes, work in columns, each containing one of four different colored cards. Beginning with the first column, place one sticker in the upper left-hand corner of each card. When finished, the cards in the first column should have four different stickers. Move to the second column and beginning with the second card down, place the stickers in the same order as in the first column, so that the last sticker is placed on the first card in that column. Move to the third column and beginning with the third card down, place the stickers in the same order as in the two previous columns, ending with the second card in the column. And finally, move to the fourth column and beginning with the last card, place the same sequence of stickers on the cards, ending with the third card down.

3. Next, beginning with the first card in the first column, draw one of four shapes (circle, pentagon, square, or triangle) in the lower left-hand corner of each card. Move to the second column and beginning with the bottom card, draw the same order of attributes. Move to the third column and begin the sequence with the second card up from the bottom. Then begin with the third card up in the last column and record the same sequence.

4. For the parts of speech, begin with the bottom card in the last column and, moving up the column, write either "verb," "noun," "adjective," or "adverb" in the lower right-hand corner of each card; or you can write four nouns, four verbs, four adjectives, or four adverbs on your cards. Moving to the third column and beginning with the second card up from the bottom, write the same sequence as was used in the last column. Go to the second column, start with the third card up, and write in the same sequence. Finally, complete the first column, starting with the top card, then dropping to the bottom card and going up the column, using the same sequence, and finishing with the second card from the top.

5. Randomly pass out the cards to your students and then announce which attribute they will be using for grouping that day.

Teacher Tips:

1. Laminate the index cards for long-term use.

2. Get enough index cards for every member of your class and fold each one in half crosswise. Inside each card, include just one attribute—a shape, sticker, part of speech, number, or color label. Limit the variety of attributes by your desired grouping size. (If you have a class of 24 and you want groups to have 4 members, use 4 each of 6 different attributes.) Each time you group, randomly pass out the cards but tell students not to open them until told to do so. Upon command, students open their cards and group themselves according to attributes.

3. Come up with your own categories of attributes that extend a part of your curriculum. For example, for geography, you might include names of continents and their countries and have students group themselves with the appropriate continents; for science, you might have them form groups according to biological classifications; etc.

Pairing Up for Learning

Explanation:

Grouping students into pairs can be an effective way to facilitate learning. Here are some motivating and creative suggestions for producing partners by matching topics in different academic areas:

- Language Arts: You Complete Me (Finish the Proverb or Compound Words)
- Poetry: Poetic Partners (Similes and Metaphors)
- Reading: Books and Authors
- Geography: States and Their Capitals
- Science: Elements and Symbols
- Math: Problems and Solutions
- Art: Artist and Work of Art
- Music: Composer and Music
- Physical Education: Sport and Equipment

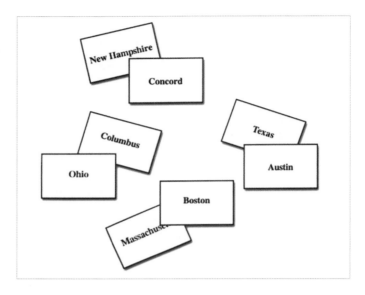

Materials:

- 3x5-inch index cards or Pair Cards reproducible for states and capitals (see pages 105-110)

Directions:

1. Prepare a set of index cards for each of the above categories that you intend to use, or reproduce those provided in the Appendix for states and capitals. If, for example, you are doing geography pairs and you have 26 students in your class:

   - Select the cards for 13 states and their capitals from the reproducibles.

   Or, to make your own:

   - Separate index cards into two piles of 13 cards each.

   - Write the names of 13 states on one set of cards.

   - Write their capitals on the remaining 13 cards.

2. When it is time to form pairs, shuffle the cards, pass them out, and have each student find his/her matching state or capital. If you have an odd number of students in your class, make a duplicate card for one of the states or capitals. This way you will have three students in one of your groups.

Teacher Tips:

1. Laminate the cards for long-term use.

2. To save time in creating these cards, let students volunteer to make them in their free time, or use this as an anchor activity (a way to keep students engaged with some other purposeful work when they finish a classroom assignment before the others).

Clock Partners

Explanation:

To encourage more active involvement among your students, instead of pairing them yourself, ask each to meet with his/her Clock Partner.

Materials:

- Clock Partners reproducible (see page 111)

Directions:

1. Give a copy of the Clock Partners reproducible to each student, and ask him/her to write his/her name in the center of the clock face.

2. Have each student ask classmates to write their names on the hours of the clock, filling each space with the name of a different student. Be sure, however, that the "owner" of the clock face writes his/her name on the same hour of the other student's clock face. In other words, if Sally signs Ann's clock face on the 10:00 space, then Ann should write her name on Sally's clock face on the 10:00 space.

3. When an activity has a sharing phase, simply ask the students to meet with, for example, their 10:00 partner. This gets students up, moving around, and interacting with others with whom they may not usually spend time.

Clock Partners

(clock diagram with handwritten names: Chris, John, Karen, Jenny, Ricki, Dave, George, Mark, Meredith, Chloe, Jennifer, Wes, and Lizz written in the center)

Teacher Tips:

1. Laminate each clock face for long-term use and have students use dry-erase or water-soluble markers when writing their names.

2. Make sure each student has a partner for each of the hours.

3. Occasionally, you might want to complete the appointments for the students so that the paired partners are on the same reading level, for example, or so a strong reader is paired with a weak reader for peer support.

Circle of Three

Explanation:

There are times when grouping students into threes is appropriate, such as for some math games and the Three-Step Interview included in this book (see page 72). The technique described below and sample reproducible show how you can practice or reinforce a skill while forming groups.

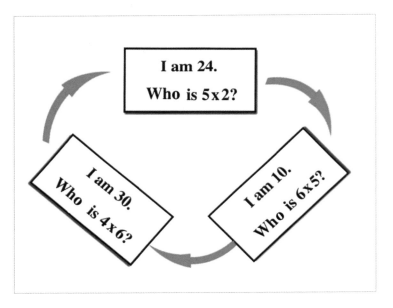

Materials

- Circle of Three reproducible (see page 112)

Directions:

1. Photocopy the reproducible on tagboard, if possible, for durability.

2. Give each student one card.

3. Model how students will use these cards to get into groups: Each student looks at the "I am..." statement on his/her card. Next, he/she looks at the "Who is...?" question on the same card.

The goal is for each student to find two people—one of whom has a card with a correct math sentence for the "I am..." and another who matches the "Who is...?" For example:

- One student has "I am 10. Who is 6x5?"

- Another student has "I am 30. Who is 4x6?"

- And another student has "I am 24. Who is 5x2?"

- These three would form a group.

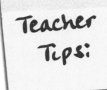

Teacher Tips:

1. Laminate the cards for long-term use.

2. If you have an extra student after grouping, put four in a group and ask two of them to work together as one member. They can take turns responding.

3. Try creating Circles of Three using other subjects, such as states and capitals. For example, one card would read: "I am Boston. Who is the capital of Colorado?" Another reads: "I am Denver. Who is the capital of Virginia?" And the third reads: "I am Richmond. Who is the capital of Massachusetts?"

Card Games for Grouping

Explanation:

A deck of playing cards can provide innumerable ways to group students. Start out using the examples described below, which will spark additional ideas of your own.

Materials:

- Deck(s) of playing cards

Directions:

1. Remove the face cards from the deck.

2. Assign the Ace a value of 1.

3. If you have 20 students, for example, in your classroom, and want to divide them into groups of 4, take out all the cards for 1 (Ace) through 5, and deal out these 20 cards to your students. Then ask your students to group by same numbers: All the 1s (Aces) get together, all the 2s, all the 3s, 4s, and 5s. If you want them to group in pairs, do the same thing but have each student find the person with the same number and same color that he/she has.

Pairs grouped by same number and color

4. Alternatively, let's say you have 24 students in your classroom and want to group them into pairs. From the deck of cards select pairs of cards that add up to some number— such as 10. For example, you could pull out the four 8s and four 2s, the four 4s and four 6s, and the four 3s and four 7s. Give each child a card and ask him/ her to find another card that, when added to his/her own card, will equal 10. This results in 12 pairs of students practicing their addition and moving around at the same time.

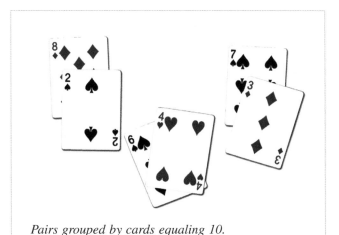

Pairs grouped by cards equaling 10.

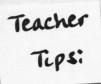

1. The variations on this theme are vast. Keep some extra decks of cards on hand so you don't always have to work with the same deck.

2. As a fun anchor activity, let the student who finishes his/her assignment early take a deck of cards and pull out the ones you need for two or three grouping activities. (An anchor activity is used during those times when you have one or more students who finish a classroom assignment ahead of the others. The intention is to keep those students engaged in something purposeful while the others finish their work.)

Selecting and Adapting Textbooks

I f you are lucky enough to be able to select your own textbooks, you may find these basic guidelines worth keeping in mind to ensure that you make the best choices. These include the following:

1. Textbooks should be reader friendly.
2. The writing style should be clear, engaging, meaningful, and thought-provoking.
3. Textbooks should cover the material in a substantive, not superficial, manner yet not rely on dense and difficult language or concepts. Vocabulary should include both challenging and familiar words.
4. Main ideas should be explicit—not implicit or embedded in the text. Headings and subheadings should be to the point, not vague or ambiguous.
5. Photographs, illustrations, diagrams, maps, charts, graphs, etc., should extend the understanding of the text and be easy to interpret. Captions should be clear and informative.
6. Illustrations and graphic elements should be positioned as close as possible to the text that they describe or support, not placed pages before or after it.
7. Color should be used to enhance comprehension and retention, not serve a purely decorative purpose.
8. The book's interior design should support and enhance the text.

   For example, the type size should not be too small and the line length of the text should not be too long. Otherwise, this could make reading slow and laborious, and cause students to lose their concentration.
9. A detailed and helpful index should be included, as well as a bibliography or recommended reading list.
10. The textbook should include information on web sites that support the content topic. An example of this would be science textbooks that show links (called SciLinks, see page 153) to sites supported and constantly updated by the National Science Teachers Association.

This chapter focuses on the needs of those who must use existing textbooks. The following strategies provide effective ways to adapt the text—and sometimes the books themselves—so that the information is more accessible to and meaningful for readers of all abilities.

Laminated Chapter Books

Explanation:

Help students who are overwhelmed by the sheer size (and weight!) of their textbooks. Simply make the books smaller by converting them into individual chapter books. This textbook change allows the students many more options when working with the text. Because pages are laminated, students can use dry-erase or water-soluble markers and write directly on the pages. This allows them to circle confusing words, underline passages, and even answer problems in the book if space allows. These books also are more manageable for students who are easily discouraged by dealing with too much material at one time.

© 2002 National Geographic Society

Materials:

- X-acto knife or box cutter
- Metal key ring
- Hole punch
- Laminating machine

Directions:

1. Using a knife, carefully remove the pages from the textbook, one chapter at a time.
2. Laminate the pages.
3. Use a hole punch to make a hole in the upper left-hand corner of each left-hand page (or right-hand corner of each right-hand page).
4. Hold the pages together with a metal key ring.

Teacher Tips:

1. Always secure administrative approval first before cutting up textbooks to create laminated chapter books.
2. Add blank, lined laminated pages to each chapter book for note taking and a separate blank page for attaching reusable Post-it notes and highlighting tape.
3. To personalize each "book," write the student's name on a luggage tag and attach it to the key ring.
4. Some students simply don't want to carry their schoolbooks home with them, and when they do, they often forget them there. So, you might consider having multiple textbooks for students—one set for school and one for home. If duplicate sets are not affordable for your school or students, it might be feasible to have at least one or two extra textbooks on hand for the student who needs special accommodations of this kind.

Smaller Is Better

Explanation:

Although similar to the previous strategy, this version will work for schools without laminating machines because you can photocopy the chapters instead. (And you don't have to cut the pages out either, if you prefer not to.) Always be sure to obtain permission first from the publisher before making any copies. (See page 113 for a sample form for securing written permission to reproduce materials under copyright.)

© 2002 National Geographic Society

Materials:

- Various binding supplies and/or equipment, such as a stapler, plastic report cover with spine, binding machine, etc.
- Clear sheets of acetate

Directions:

1. Photocopy the textbook, one chapter at a time, making a copy for each student needing this accommodation.

2. Use a method of your choice for binding the pages together.

3. Add two sheets of acetate between each pair of pages for making changes (see Eliminate Unnecessary Information, page 27).

Teacher Tips:

1. Always secure permission from the textbook publisher first before reproducing any copyrighted material.

2. Suggest to your students that these easily transportable chapter books are ideal to read when they are waiting for the school bus, while riding the bus, or during other transitional times.

3. Some schools have removed lockers for safety reasons, but this requires students to carry all their books throughout the day. Many people feel that carrying a lot of weight in a backpack could have detrimental effects, so this strategy might have health benefits too.

Textbook Talk-back Notes

Substitute Headings and Subheadings in the Form of Questions

Explanation:

Easily understandable (explicit) headings and sub-headings can trigger prior knowledge, help students read for purpose and make predictions, improve reading comprehension, and conserve valuable learning time (see also Textbook Look-back strategy, page 98). Headings and subheadings that are vague and are not clearly expressed (implicit) may confuse some students and hinder their reading the text. Rewrite those that need clarification, turning them into questions.

Old Heading

Rewritten heading on mailing label or opaque tape

Materials:

- Tape and/or mailing labels (permanent and/or nonpermanent; opaque and/or transparent)

Directions:

1. Preview the chapter ahead of time, looking carefully for confusing headings and subheadings, and then rewrite those that might hinder students' comprehension.

2. Cover the existing heading/subheading with nonpermanent opaque tape or a label.

3. Write new wording directly on the tape or label.

Teacher Tips:

1. Computer mailing labels work well for permanent changes.

2. You can help your students become independent learners by letting them see what the original wording was and how it was changed. One way to do this is by using tape and writing above or below the heading.

3. You can also use this as an After-Reading Strategy by having your students choose the main ideas from the readings and rewrite the headings themselves.

Eliminate Unnecessary Information

Explanation:

When some students read expository text, they have a difficult time determining what is germane and what is extraneous. This strategy, which also has proven helpful to poor readers, provides an easy way to omit text that is unimportant. Eventually, your goal is to reach the point with your students at which they can eliminate the unnecessary text themselves. Struggling students, of course, may not be able to do this, so you may have to continue to mark their pages.

Materials:

- Plastic page protectors
- Dry-erase or water-soluble marker

Directions:

1. Place a plastic page protector, cut down to size, over the textbook page. Keep one corner of the sheet intact to hold it in place.

2. Make alignment marks on each corner of the plastic sheet to allow for removing it and replacing it in the correct position. If you are doing this for a student, make sure you number each plastic sheet.

3. Use a marker to cross out text details deemed unnecessary.

Before

After

Teacher Tips:

1. Use a permanent marker if you want to make these changes permanently.

2. Clear sheets of acetate also work well. Use paper clips or nonpermanent tape to fasten the sheet to the page.

3. Model this strategy for your students, using an overhead transparency of a section of the text. Once the students are confident with how this strategy works, have them remove what they feel is "fluff," or unimportant information, in another part of the text.

Textbook Talk-back Notes

Circle and Box Math Problems

Explanation:

This organizational strategy helps your students reduce careless math errors when computing with mixed operations by focusing on one step at a time.

Materials:

- Nonpermanent tape
- Paper clips
- Sheet of acetate or plastic page protector
- Dry-erase or water-soluble marker

Directions:

1. Use tape or paper clips to attach a sheet of acetate to the textbook page. (A plastic page protector cut down to size also works well and doesn't require fastening.)

2. Use a marker to box the multiplication examples and circle the division examples.

3. Have your students do all the multiplication examples first and correct them.

4. Have your students complete all the division examples and correct them.

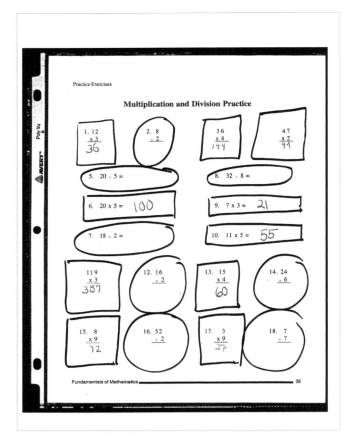

Teacher Tips:

1. Use a marker or highlighting tape to color code operation signs or specific words in the directions.

2. Use this strategy also with addition and subtraction.

3. Copy the text page and allow students to box and circle the actual problems themselves. Secure written permission first, using the form on page 113, before reproducing any copyrighted material.

Large-Print Textbooks

Explanation:

Some students experience visual difficulty reading the small print in a textbook. Providing them with a copy of the text in a larger point size will not only make the content more visually accessible but also make it easier for these students to modify the text with highlighting tape, etc.

Large-print edition

Normal textbook print

Materials:

- Textbook with 20-point type

Directions:

1. Check first with your textbook publisher to see if the book is available in a large-print edition.

2. If it is not available, request permission from the publisher to make enlarged copies of the textbook. Enlargements can be made on a photocopier using 11x17-inch paper and setting the magnification to 1.25 to 1.5.

Teacher Tips:

1. Be sure to protect students from the potential stigma of using material that differs substantially from that of the rest of the class. Openly discuss during class meetings the fact that some students will be using different materials that work best for their learning needs. Encourage your students to recognize and support differences.

2. See page 149 for ordering information about large-print textbooks.

3. Try to find large-print textbooks that are published in color.

Textbook Adaptation Plan

Explanation:

Create a three-part textbook adaptation plan with your students' input to assist those who are having a lot of difficulty with textbook learning. These step-by-step forms are legally nonbinding but are used in good faith.

Materials:

- Copies of Textbook Adaptation Plan reproducible (see pages 114-116)

Directions:

1. Make copies of the forms that are applicable for your student(s).

2. Fill in the forms with your students' participation.

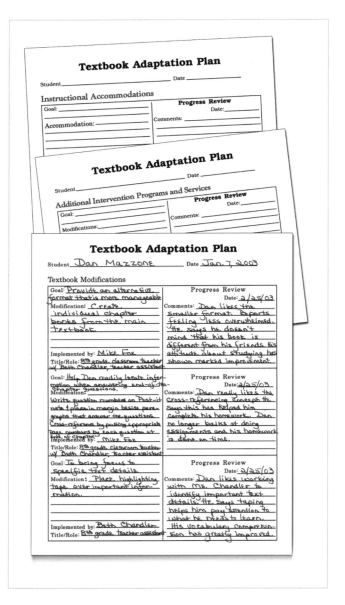

Teacher Tips:

1. You will sometimes use only one or two of the forms as opposed to all three.

2. To keep communications open, you may want to send copies of these home with the student so parents can see the adaptations that are being made for their child.

Before-Reading Strategies

In order for students to fully comprehend content-area textbooks, they must think about what they already know regarding the topic in the textbook and set a purpose for reading. To set a purpose for reading, students think ahead about what they are going to get out of their reading. For example, are they going be informed or entertained? As a teacher, your role is to engage students in a variety of before-reading strategies designed to help them prepare to read the textbook. Activating and building upon students' prior knowledge about a subject, helping students set a purpose for reading, introducing content-area vocabulary, and motivating students to want to read the textbook are all examples of what you can do to help. your students get ready to read.

Concept Map: A New Version of KWL

INDIVIDUAL   SMALL GROUP
PAIRS   WHOLE GROUP

Explanation:

The major purpose of KWL (What I Know, What I Want to Know [or What I Wonder], and What I Learned) is to activate students' prior knowledge about textbook material before they read the text. It also helps guide them during reading as they think about what they want to know—or what they wonder—about the topic. After reading, it helps them organize what they learned. Because this is such a popular strategy, it often becomes a work sheet that students fill out individually before reading. This approach can be more powerful if you invite "collaborative learning" while using it. In other words, by making the work sheet interactive (triggering a discussion) and using it as a graphic organizer, you can increase your students' motivation and interest in the content of the textbook. In addition, struggling students benefit from the discussion with others. Students can learn to see each other as sources of information. This strategy is particularly helpful to students who tend to begin reading without even thinking about the topic.

Materials:

- Concept Map reproducible (see page 117).

Directions:

1. Divide students into small groups and give each group a copy of the concept map.

2. Discuss with the whole class what they "think they know" about the topic and ask each small group to list those items in the circle on their concept map.

3. Facilitate whole class discussion about what categories of information students wonder about, or what they would like to learn about as they study the text. Then ask each small group to write these categories on the lines projecting out from the circle.

4. Have students use the categories of information they wonder about or want to know about to create a concept map that serves as a visual tool, helping them integrate what they knew before reading and what they learned as a result of their reading.

5. After they read, ask each group to finish filling in their concept map.

6. With their concept map, have each group report to the whole class what they originally thought they knew about the topic, what they wanted to know, and finally, what they learned.

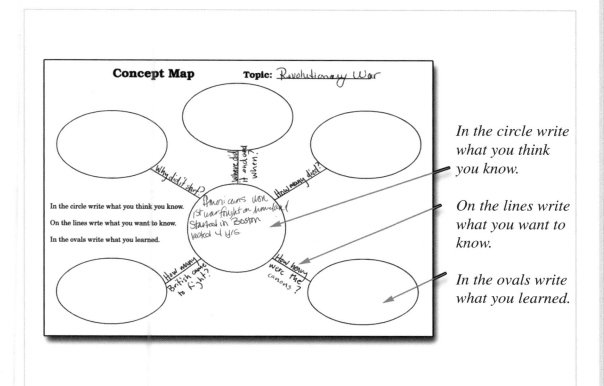

Concept Map   Topic: Revolutionary War

In the circle write what you think you know.

On the lines write what you want to know.

In the ovals write what you learned.

In the circle write what you think you know.

On the lines wrte what you want to know.

In the ovals write what you learned.

Americans won
1st war fought on homeland
Started in Boston
lasted 4 yrs

Why did it start?

Where did it and and when?

How many died?

How many British came to fight?

How heavy were the canons?

Teacher Tips:

1. Circulate among student groups as they work with this graphic organizer so you can note their misconceptions about a topic and use them for a later discussion.

2. Ask students in each group to choose a "reporter" to describe to the classroom what they thought they knew, what they wanted to know—or wondered about—and what they learned.

Compacting Textbook Chapters

Explanation:

Compacting the curriculum is a process in which you begin by establishing what the learning objectives are going to be for a particular subject, then pretest or assess your students to find out how much they already know about the learning objectives. Based on their prior mastery, you compress (or compact) the volume of work they are required to do to include only those skills or concepts that they have not yet mastered. This allows students to extend their learning through individual or small group projects, while you teach the content and skills to other students who have not yet learned the material.

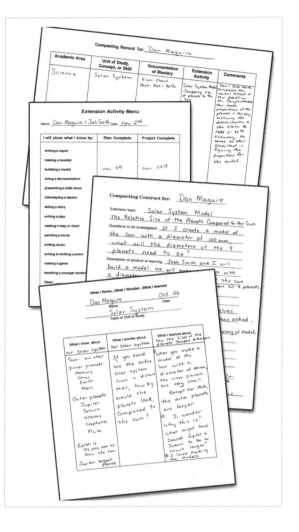

Materials:

- What I Know (KWL) Chart • Extension Activity Menu
- Compacting Contract • Compacting Record
    (see reproducibles, pages 118-121)

Directions:

1. Assess students' prior knowledge and/or skills through a chapter pretest or a KWL chart. This chart has the phrase "What I wonder about" instead of the traditional "What I want to know." When students write about what they wonder about a topic, it helps identify their areas of interest and possible questions to address in their projects.

2. Allow students who show sufficient mastery to choose from a menu of extension activities. (The "K" or "What I know about" helps you determine if a student has sufficiently mastered the material.) The independent or small-group study is usually an extension of the theme you are currently studying.

3. Once you and your students have agreed on an activity, have them create a rubric to show different levels of mastery.

4. Ask each of these students to sign a contract, agreeing to a set of rules for an independent or small-group project and for behavioral expectations. While you work with the rest of the class, contract students work on their own extension activity.

5. If a student breaks the rules of the contract, he/she loses the privilege of working independently.

Example of When, Why, and How to Compact the Curriculum

Let's say your class is about to begin a study of the solar system. One week prior to starting this unit, ask each student to use a KWL chart to list what he/she already knows about this topic in the "K" column of his/her chart. Also ask your students to write their questions in the "W" column, which asks what they wonder about the solar system. As you review the responses, you may find that two students' KWL charts indicate mastery of the content, as outlined in the unit's objectives. On their charts, the students accurately named and described the planets, and shared other interesting facts about comets, asteroids, meteors, etc. It is obvious that these students already know the content the class is about to investigate, so you may decide to compact the curriculum on the solar system for these two. Instead of studying what they already know, let them extend their learning on a specific topic that relates to the solar system. This way they can apply the facts they know to a meaningful project. Then they might meet with your teacher-directed group only when a lesson is offered on a topic they have not yet mastered.

To begin, meet with the two students to identify an area of interest that aligns with the unit's objectives. Have them use the Extension Activity Menu to choose a project that will demonstrate their learning. Say the students choose "building a model" from the list and choose to study the size of each planet relative to that of the sun. They decide to begin by building a miniature model of the sun (100 mm in diameter), which will serve as the point of reference for the entire solar system. Each planet's size will be based on that of the model of the sun.

Next, review the Compacting Contract with the students. Make sure the topic, the product, the rules, and a rubric are listed and agreed upon. With the solar system for their model, let's say the students use the following criteria to evaluate their project:

The objective is to create a mathematically accurate miniature model of the solar system that shows the size of each planet relative to that of the sun. The following percentages will serve as the rubric's criteria for success:

4 = 90-100% accuracy   2 = 70-79% accuracy

3 = 80-89% accuracy   1 = Below 70% accuracy

When the model is complete, the students decide how and to whom to present it. The relative size of the sun and the planets is measured and shared by the students. After the presentation, you enter the information on each student's Compacting Record sheet.

Teacher Tip:

1. Explain to students that sometimes there will be "no contract days." These occur when you have special lessons for the entire class or an activity in which everyone participates.

Pros, Cons, and What I Wonder

Explanation:

Remaining engaged with text is difficult for some students, yet necessary for comprehension. Used both before and after reading, this strategy helps set a purpose for reading and supports an understanding of both informational and fictional texts. An example of using this strategy with a study of water as a natural resource might be a question like: "What if it never rained again?"

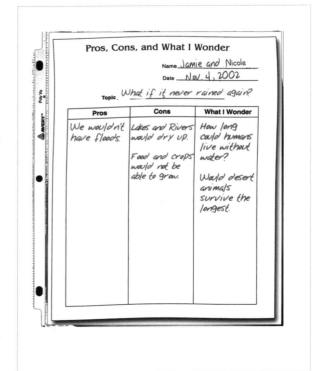

Materials:

- Dry-erase or water-soluble markers
- Clear plastic page protectors
- Pros, Cons, and What I Wonder chart (see page 122)

Directions:

1. Decide if students will work individually, as partners, or in small groups.

2. Make copies of the chart and give a copy to each student or group.

3. Explain to students that they will have three minutes to brainstorm all the "pros," or positive things, they can think of about their topic, and then write these under the "Pros" column on their chart.

4. Next, tell them they will have three minutes to brainstorm all the "cons," or negative aspects, and write these under the "Cons" column on their chart.

5. Have a class discussion about the students' brainstorming lists.

6. After the discussion, ask students to write any questions they wonder about in the "What I Wonder" column.

7. Finally, have them read the text.

1. Prepare the charts in advance.

2. Place charts in page protectors so they can be reused by simply wiping them off after each lesson.

3. For a post-reading activity, have another class discussion on their thoughts about the pros and cons they listed before reading. Students' questions in the "What I Wonder" column can lead to effective extensions or further research on the topic.

Guess the Word

Textbook Talk-back
Notes

Explanation:

Guess the Word is a non-threatening way to get students involved in figuring out new content words by having them use structural and contextual clues. Students enjoy trying to guess what the words mean before they see a sentence with clues because there is no right or wrong answer at that point.

Materials:

- Prefixes and Suffixes reproducible (see page 123)

Directions:

1. Select vocabulary words from the text to be studied. Give them to the students before they read their textbooks.

2. Have students work in pairs and use each word's structure (prefix, suffix) to try to guess the meaning of the words. Share student responses aloud.

3. Provide the words again to the students, but this time present them in a rich context so they will be able to use the context clues to figure out the meanings.

4. Have students verify meanings with dictionaries.

1. Pre-select the vocabulary words to use and then write each in a sentence with a rich context so that students can figure out the meaning.

2. Turn this into a game by having students from different groups read their definitions of the same word, then having other groups vote on which they think is closest to the real meaning. See which group has the "best" definition most often.

3. Although the reproducible (Prefixes and Suffixes) won't always be used for this particular strategy, it may come in handy at other times when students are trying to figure out the meanings of certain words.

Vocabulary Index Cards

Explanation:

Having students create their own set of vocabulary index cards allows them to do more than just look up a word in the dictionary. It allows them to represent the meaning of each word in four different ways. Students can also use their cards to study for content-area vocabulary tests.

Materials:

- Index cards of different sizes

Directions:

1. Give students a list of content-area words that are critical to their understanding of the textbook passage they are going to read.

2. Provide index cards of several different sizes for the students, giving each one a choice as to the size card he/she would prefer to use.

3. Have students write each vocabulary word in the center of a card—one word per index card.

4. Ask students to write a working definition of the word in the upper left-hand corner of the card. They can look it up in the dictionary first and then use their own words.

5. Ask students to write a synonym for the word in the top right-hand corner.

6. Ask students to write the word's part of speech in the bottom left-hand corner.

7. Have students draw a picture in the lower right-hand corner that shows they understand the word's meaning.

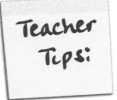

Teacher Tips:

1. Ask students to preview the textbook passage and select their own words with which to create their cards.

2. In some cases, a word will not have a synonym. Tell students to write "N/A" (not applicable) in those instances.

Taped Vocabulary Words

Textbook Talk-back
Notes

Explanation:

Lack of vocabulary understanding is frequently cited as the prime reason many students struggle with reading comprehension. This strategy provides an auditory tool for students who learn best this way.

Materials:

- Audiocassette tapes
- Audiocassette player

Directions:

1. Select important vocabulary words from the textbook readings and record their meanings on audiocassette tapes.

2. Encourage students to use headphones to listen to the audiocassettes at home or during transition times in their day.

tab

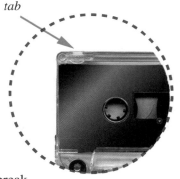

1. Ten-minute audiocassettes work well for recording vocabulary words and require less rewinding and fast-forwarding for students than longer tapes.

Teacher Tips:

2. To keep from inadvertently recording over a tape that you want to preserve, break off one of the tabs on the top edge of the plastic case. Make sure you remove the correct tab by turning the tape so that you are looking at the side that has been recorded on. Then break off (or push inside the case) the tab on the top left side of the tape.

Talking Flash Cards

INDIVIDUAL PAIRS **SMALL GROUP** **WHOLE GROUP**

Explanation:

Audio flash cards are an effective way to teach and reinforce new vocabulary words. They can be used individually, in pairs, or in small groups.

Materials:

- The CardMaster® and ancillary products (see page 149)

Directions:

1. Write vocabulary words, and sentences using the words in context, on the print side of the blank recorder cards.

2. On each card, record the pronunciation of the word and also record its definition.

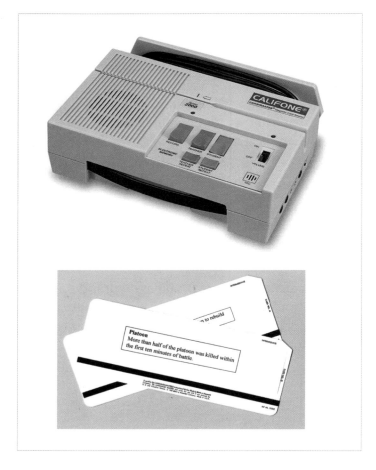

Teacher Tip:

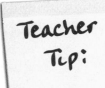

1. This anchor activity makes a great self-sustaining listening center for individuals, pairs, or small groups. (An anchor activity is an activity a student can perform so he/she is engaged while the teacher is working with other students. It is a way of "anchoring" a student to something productive, like reading a book or working in a center, until the teacher is again available for the student or entire class.)

Card Master® and flash card images reproduced by permission of Califone International, Inc.

Online Vocabulary Help

Textbook Talk-back Notes

Explanation:

Students can now take advantage of free online references, such as the Merriam-Webster web site, to help them with unfamiliar new words. The audio portion of this site is particularly helpful to students who would have trouble sounding out the words and to English Language Learner (ELL) students.

Materials:

- Computer with sound card and speakers

Directions:

1. Provide students with a list of terms they may have difficulty with in their textbook reading.

2. Have students go to www.Merriam-Webster.com, where they can type in each word.

3. Have students click on the audio symbol to hear the correct pronunciation of the word.

4. Vary assignments by asking students to retrieve different kinds of information for each word, such as:

    a. the definition

    b. a synonym

    c. the word in a sentence

    d. the plural form of the word

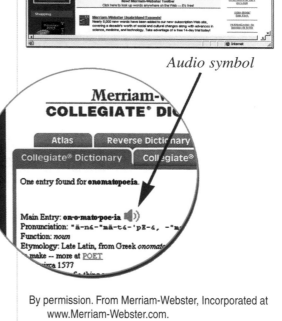

Audio symbol

By permission. From Merriam-Webster, Incorporated at www.Merriam-Webster.com.

Teacher Tip:

1. This anchor activity (see previous page for definition) works well as a computer-based vocabulary center.

List-Group-Label

INDIVIDUAL   **SMALL GROUP**
PAIRS   WHOLE GROUP

Explanation:

List-Group-Label allows students to discuss and manipulate words as a way to prepare to read the textbook. Students examine a list of words taken from a text and look for relationships between them. Then they group the words and identify the unifying concept for each grouping they create. This helps students access background knowledge, stimulates their thinking, and prepares them to read purposefully. It also helps them learn how to categorize and classify information.

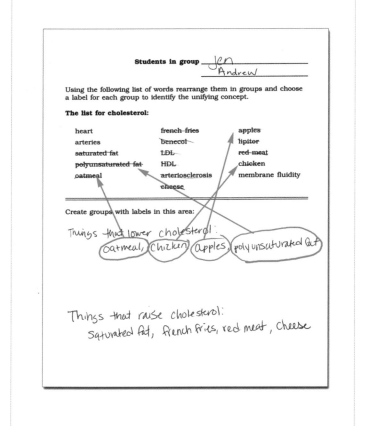

Directions:

1. List 15 to 20 words from the textbook selection and give a copy of the list to each student.

2. Have students group and label the words, identifying the labels or categories they are using.

3. Ask students to share their grouping and labeling of words with at least one other student or pair of students in the class.

4. Have students read the material in the textbook and then revisit their grouping and labeling to discuss any misconceptions.

Teacher Tips:

1. Instead of selecting the words yourself, show the students a picture from the text or a video on the subject and ask them to generate a list of words related to the picture/video.

2. If students are already familiar with the topic, they can generate the list of words without any visual prompting.

Anticipation Guide

Explanation:

The Anticipation Guide is an excellent strategy for motivating students to read the textbook by activating prior knowledge and setting purposes for content-area reading. Students engage in a lively discussion by reacting to statements before reading.

Anticipation Guide
LIONS

Agree	Disagree	
☐	☑	1. Lions are not meat eaters.
☑	☐	2. A family of lions is called a pride.
☑	☐	3. Lions live like kings.
☐	☑	4. Most of today's lions live in South America.
☑	☐	5. Baby lions weigh over ten pounds at birth.
☐	☑	6. It is easy for a lion to survive.

Directions:

1. Write 6 to 10 statements (fact, fiction, opinion, or any combination of these) regarding a topic or a section of the reading your students will be doing in their textbook.

2. Give each student a copy of the statements and ask him/her to indicate with a check mark whether he/she agrees or disagrees with each statement. Accept all answers; there are no right or wrong answers at this point.

3. Activate a lively discussion around the statements and the students' answers. One way to do this would be to ask for a show of hands about how they voted on each statement.

4. Follow with another discussion about why they voted the way they did. Encourage students to give reasons why they support or challenge other students' answers.

Teacher Tips:

1. To prepare an Anticipation Guide, you need to identify major concepts from the textbook selection that students will be reading and then craft the statements accordingly.

2. After students read the selection from their textbook, have them revisit the statements in their Anticipation Guide and decide if they have changed their minds about any of the statements. If so, ask them to note the page number from the text that supports each of their responses.

3. For a Pair-and-Share activity, have each of a pair of students create his/her own individual statements for an Anticipation Guide. Then have them trade and fill out each other's guides. Afterward they can discuss why they made the choices they did.

Textbook Talk-back Notes

Timed Responses

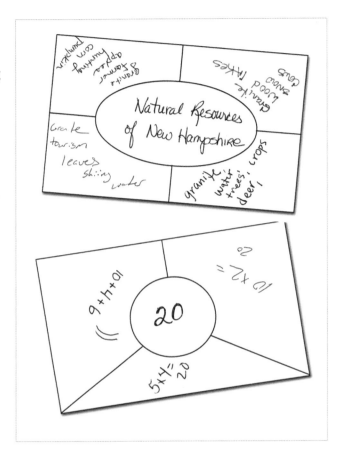

Explanation:

This group-response technique can be used before reading to summarize prior knowledge or after reading to summarize what has been learned. It can also be used both before and after to help students monitor their learning progress.

Materials:

- Large sheets of paper (11x17-inch size works well)
- Pencils or markers
- Timer

Directions:

1. Divide your class into small groups and give each group paper and pencils.

2. Write the prompt or question in a circle or oval at the center of each group's paper.

3. Divide the paper around the center circle into sections equal to the number of students in the group.

4. Announce the group guidelines:

   - Respectful rules
   - Response time
   - Discussion format and time

5. Explain that students are to write individually as much as they can in response to the prompt until a time's-up signal is given. (Use a signal to begin and end.) Times for this exercise can vary. Depending on the task and the group, allow one minute or more.

6. Allow a one-minute reflect-and-review time for students to look over their responses.

7. Finally, have them share responses, looking for commonalities and new information.

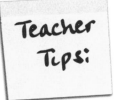

1. When first using this technique, be sure to model and practice with a simple prompt, such as "Things That Begin with the Letter 'S,'" so all students can focus on the process and feel successful with the task.

2. Tier the questions from the textbook or tier the complexity of the prompts, then assign students to groups based on their skills or concept-attainment. (Tiering refers to matching or tailoring the instructional or readiness level of the student to the complexity of the material.)

3. Ask a representative from each group to share the group's prompt and their favorite two or three responses.

Cloze Activity

Textbook Talk-back
Notes

Explanation:

This is a prediction and purpose-setting strategy that prepares students to read the textbook. It functions as an advanced organizer as well as a way to assess the prior knowledge of the students while piquing their interest in what they are about to read in the textbook.

Close the Cloze

The term for arranging things into categories according to established _criteria_ is called classification. The science of naming, classifying, and identifying organisms is called _anthropology_. For example, the only creatures that have six legs and two wings are _arthropods_. The people who determine the criteria by which groups are to be recognized are called _anthropologists_.

Directions:

1. Choose a paragraph from the textbook selection that students are going to read. Copy it, omitting some of the interesting words and leaving blanks where the words were.

2. Make copies of the resulting paragraph for your students.

3. Divide the class into pairs and give each pair a copy of the paragraph with the blanks.

4. Ask each pair of students to fill in the blanks with words they think would work in the paragraph. Each pair of students is "closing the cloze" paragraph by filling in word choices that make sense.

5. Have each pair of students read their paragraph so that the entire class can compare and contrast the different choices made.

Teacher Tips:

1. Select a paragraph from the textbook before students have read it and rewrite the content, leaving blanks for students to complete.

2. Choose interesting words to delete as well as words that have several possible substitutions so students can have many choices for a word that works.

3. Refer to Chapter 1 for quick and easy grouping strategies.

Greet and Go

INDIVIDUAL
PAIRS

SMALL GROUP
WHOLE GROUP

Explanation:

Greet and Go is an interactive way to get students to use their background knowledge to make predictions about what they are going to read and to set purposes for reading the textbook.

Materials:

• Index cards of any size

Directions:

1. Divide students into groups of three to four.

2. Give each student one index card on which you have written a different phrase or sentence from the textbook passage the students are about to read.

3. Ask the students to circulate around the classroom and read their cards to each other but not make notes.

4. After about five minutes, have the students return to their groups.

5. Ask each group to jointly write a prediction on what the textbook passage will be about, based on what they remember from their interactions with others while milling around the room. Have each group start their prediction with the words "We think…" and write it on a sheet of paper.

6. Call on each group to read their statement and explain their group's reason for their prediction.

Teacher Tips:

1. Create the set of index cards with the excerpted phrases or sentences ahead of time.

2. Ask each group to select a "spokesperson" to explain their prediction.

3. Refer to Chapter 1 for quick and easy grouping strategies.

Word Toss

INDIVIDUAL **SMALL GROUP**
PAIRS   **WHOLE GROUP**

Textbook Talk-back
Notes

Explanation:

Word Toss engages students in actively predicting major ideas from content material and involves them in setting purposes for textbook reading. This strategy also allows students to become familiar with key vocabulary.

Materials:

- Pieces of acetate

Directions:

1. Write 7 to 10 important words or terms on separate pieces of acetate. Place them randomly on the overhead so they appear to have been tossd there. For example, a health textbook passage about the body might include: energy, arteries, blood, heart, lungs, stomach, body system. If you are using unfamiliar terms, introduce them to the students with a brief explanation.

2. Arrange students in small groups (or let them group themselves).

3. Ask each group to choose some or all of the words on the screen and write a sentence with them, predicting how the terms might be related to each other, based on what they are about to read. For example: "Your heart pumps blood into your arteries, lungs, and stomach and gives your body system energy." (Do not worry about the accuracy of the statement at this point.) Have each group read their sentence aloud.

4. Have students read the passage in the textbook and check the accuracy of their predictions, revising their sentences, if necessary, to be consistent with their reading of the textbook.

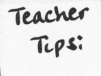

1. Prepare Word Toss by first identifying major concepts from the textbook selection that students will be reading. Then choose key terms and/or phrases to "toss" onto the overhead screen.

2. You can direct students to use all the words or let them choose four or five from the word toss when writing their sentences.

Thinking Aloud: A Fix-Up Strategy

Explanation:

A good way to help students comprehend their textbook readings is by think-aloud modeling. This allows them to "see" inside your head and learn how to apply different strategies to various problem areas. Reinforcing with repeated modeling and guided practice will enable students to eventually "own" the strategies and use them independently.

"One thing I do when I am confused is…"

Directions:

1. Choose a passage from a textbook to read aloud to your students.

2. Describe to your students what you are thinking about as you read the text. For example, you might read:

   "Lizards are really amazing! They can live in lots of different places and can change color for all sorts of reasons. Some lizards are five or six feet in length and can even eat rats, frogs, and birds."

   After you read the first sentence, you might say, "I don't think lizards are amazing at all. I think they're kind of gross! So I begin to wonder why the textbook author would say that, and I keep on reading to see if I can find out. This is a fix-up strategy for me because if I keep reading, many times the author clears up my confusion."

3. Another think-aloud strategy might focus on an unfamiliar word. After you read a passage to the students, you might say, "I'm not sure what that word means. I'm going to reread it in the sentence to see if maybe I can get the meaning by thinking about how it's used with the other words in the sentence. If I'm still confused, I'm going to need to look up the word immediately or make a note to check out its meaning later." This think-aloud modeling would also work with a confusing phrase or sentence.

Teacher Tips:

1. Plan your think-aloud modeling before reading the textbook passages to the class. Often teachers' editions provide the exact wording for teachers to use.

2. Once the think-aloud strategies have been modeled several times, stop a student during or after the reading of a textbook passage and ask him/her to think aloud for you and the rest of the class. Have the student point out specific places in the text where he/she had to pause because of difficulty with comprehending the text, and ask what he/she thought and did at those times.

Overhead Textbook Visuals

INDIVIDUAL   SMALL GROUP
PAIRS   **WHOLE GROUP**

Explanation:

Using visual aids of pertinent textbook charts, maps, and graphs helps students interpret and understand the data.

Materials:

- Photocopier machine (preferably color)
- Overhead projector and screen

Directions:

1. Copy some of the important charts, maps, and graphs from the textbook to make into overhead transparencies. Enlarge the images if necessary. Secure written permission from the publisher before copying any copyrighted material (see sample permission form, page 113).

2. Use the overhead to have a whole class discussion on how to interpret and summarize the information.

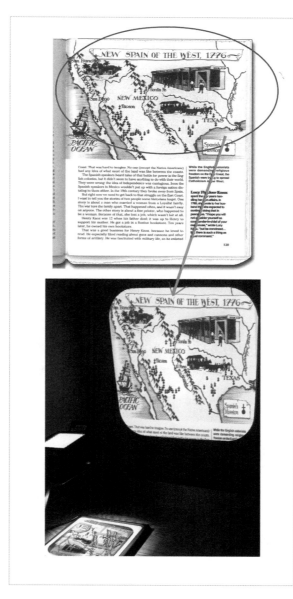

Textbook Talk-back Notes

Teacher Tips:

1. Photocopied enlargements of the charts, maps, and graphs work well as teaching posters for small-group instruction.

2. Most copy shops require written permission from the publisher before reproducing copyrighted materials.

From A HISTORY OF US: FROM COLONIES TO COUNTRY (VOL 3) by Joy Hakim, © 1993 by Joy Hakim. Used by permission of Oxford University Press, Inc.

Clear Up Math Visuals

Explanation:

Many math word problems could be much more accessible to students if they were supported by clear, pertinent visuals rather than accompanied by distracting or decorative illustrations. If your math textbook is lacking in this area, help your students create their own visual aids.

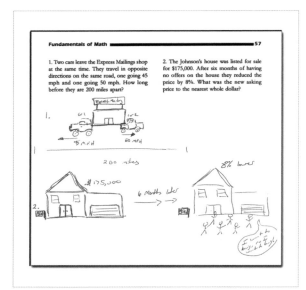

Materials:

- Sheets of acetate
- Dry-erase or water-soluble markers
- Overhead projector

Directions:

1. Provide students with dry-erase or water-soluble markers and sheets of acetate.

2. Before students start the word problems, work as a whole group by reading through the problem and having students discuss appropriate visuals.

3. Have each student write the appropriate problem number on his/her sheet and illustrate the word problem.

4. Project each on the overhead and discuss with the class.

Teacher Tips:

1. This activity works well even for nonartistic students. Remind them that their drawings need only to support the text and can be very simple. Almost all word problems that are based on the Distance=Rate x Time formula fall into one of these illustrated categories (right). Getting students to recognize which situation the problem is describing helps them write the correct equation for solving the problem.

2. When choosing textbooks be sure to note whether the illustrations support the text. Check out Singapore Math textbooks, which are known worldwide for the excellent match they provide between each math problem and the accompanying illustration. (See page 152 for information on these books.)

Estimating Math Answers

Textbook Talk-back
Notes

Explanation:

Predicting in math takes the form of estimating answers to problems. By estimating answers first your students learn to always look at their answers to see if they make sense.

Math Answer Estimates

Problem Number	Estimate	Actual Answer
1.	100	87
2.	75	83
3.	35	35
4.	120	118
5.	20	20
6.	10	10
7	85	92
8.	40	40
9.	300	293
10.	410	392
11.	150	150
12.	200	200
13.	175	184
14	250	250

Materials:

* Math Answer Estimates reproducible (see page 124)

Directions:

1. Start by reading the problems and estimating the answers as a whole group activity. Share some of the things you consider when you are coming up with an estimate.

2. Have students complete the chart prior to doing problems.

3. After the problems have been completed, ask your students to go back and compare the actual answers to their estimates.

Teacher Tip:

1. To refine their estimating skills and to keep the "Estimate" column within reason, add one more column for the students to fill in, showing the difference between the actual answer and the estimate. You might also have them total this additional column to see who has the smallest totals and is therefore the best estimator.

...th Answer Estimates

...er	Estimate	Actual Answer	Difference between estimate and answer
	100	87	13
	75	83	−8
	35	35	0
	120	118	2
	20	20	0
	10	10	0
	85	92	−7
	40	40	0
	300	293	7
	410	392	18
		150	0
		200	

Pointer/Signal Words and Text Structure

Explanation:

Pre-reading a textbook chapter, as described below, is an effective study technique for helping students gain an overall impression of its contents. It enables them to get ready to think and stay focused. Before your students actually try it themselves, however, you should model this process yourself, thinking out loud as you do it.

Materials:

• Pointer/Signal Words reproducible (see page 125)

Directions:

1. Model and practice the following steps with your students.

2. Have them begin by reading the title of the textbook chapter. Then ask them to read the introduction or the first paragraph of the chapter to get an idea of what the content is about.

3. Provide each student with a copy of the Pointer/Signal Words so they can determine the type of text structure used.

4. Ask your students to read the first sentence of each paragraph in the chapter. Many times the first sentence will let the reader know what the paragraph is about. Sometimes, however, the first sentence is just an attention grabber. If that is the case, have them read the second sentence in that paragraph to see if they can get the central thought of the paragraph.

5. Have your students examine any pictures, graphs, maps, diagrams, tables, or other visual aids provided in the chapter. These are usually included to point out what is important in the chapter.

6. Ask your students to read the last paragraph or chapter summary in order to gain an understanding of the chapter's main points.

7. If end-of-chapter questions are included, have students read them and keep them in mind while reading the chapter. This will keep them actively involved in their reading.

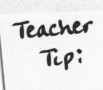

Teacher Tip:

1. Enhance the process of pre-reading by having an oral classroom discussion.

From A HISTORY OF US: WAR, PEACE, AND ALL THAT JAZZ (VOL 9) by Joy Hakim, © 1995 by Joy Hakim. Used by permission of Oxford University Press, Inc.

R.S.V.P. (READ-SUMMARIZE-VERIFY-PREDICTION CORRECTIONS)

INDIVIDUAL PAIRS   SMALL GROUP WHOLE GROUP

Explanation:

R.S.V.P. is used to activate students' prior knowledge as well as assess their understanding of a topic. This strategy promotes active reading (which means they are thinking about what they are reading) and motivates students by having them predict what they think the text will be about.

Directions:

1. Give students a list of 10 to 12 words, terms, or phrases in the order in which they appear in the textbook passage they are going to read.

2. Have each work independently or with a partner to think of connections or clues in the list and then write a possible summary of the text. Students must keep the words in the order in which they received them when writing their versions of the textbook passage.

3. Ask the students to read the textbook and compare it to their versions.

4. Have them verify and/or correct their initial predictions by rewriting their summaries after they have read the text.

Textbook Talk-back Notes

R.S.V.P

Name: Timmy Selby

1. George Washington
2. Potomac River
3. Oct. 1791
4. Nation's capital
5. chose an area of low wetlands and woods
6. building
7. easily get to
8. measured the land
9. planned the city's streets and buildings
10. capitol
11. where lawmakers meet

Write a possible summary of the text you will soon be reading using all of the words in the above list. When writing you need to use the words in your summary in the exact order they are listed above.

George Washington crossed the Potomac river in Oct 1791 to get to the nations capital. He chose an area of low wetlands and wood to build a building where he could easily get to food. He then measured the land and planned the city streets and buildings. This soon became the capital where lawmakers meet. — The end

Teacher Tips:

1. Prepare your list of words, terms, or phrases ahead of time.

2. If you want your students to work in pairs, refer to Chapter 1 for quick and easy grouping strategies.

Highlighting Text

Explanation:

Using color on specific areas of the text helps students focus their attention on specific details. Because highlighting tape is a transparent tape that comes in a variety of colors, it can be used to indicate different categories within the same page. Also, the tape's special adhesive allows for easy removal without damage to the textbook or paper, thus making the tape reusable.

From A HISTORY OF US: WAR, PEACE, AND ALL THAT JAZZ (VOL 9) by Joy Hakim, © 1995 by Joy Hakim. Used by permission of Oxford University Press, Inc.

Materials:

- Highlighting tape in various colors and widths (see page 150)

Directions:

1. Determine which width tape will work best for the size of the print you will be highlighting.

2. Decide what elements of the text you wish to highlight. You might choose one color to highlight new vocabulary words, one color to focus attention on important people, and another color for important events.

3. Initially, do the highlighting yourself to model the technique, but then give the tape to the students so they can highlight words, phrases, clauses, parts of speech, or other information based on a code you provide to them. For example:

Highlighting Code

Use yellow tape to identify nonrestrictive clauses.
Use green to identify restrictive clauses.
Use blue to identify prepositional phrases.

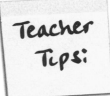

Teacher Tips:

1. Highlighting tape is also available in sheets that can be cut to size.

2. The tape can be written on with just about any pen or marker to further illuminate words and phrases.

3. Provide students with a laminated sheet of tagboard or a manila folder for storing their strips of tape for future use.

4. An alternative to highlighting tape is the erasable highlighting marker, which students can use and then erase from the textbook pages when they finish studying each chapter.

During-Reading Strategies

S tudents need to focus and concentrate while they are reading. Your role during this phase is to help them learn how to process the information in their textbooks so that their minds do not wander. In other words, they need to stay actively involved while reading. The various strategies in this chapter help students organize the information and engage in intentional thinking as they read.

Keep-Your-Place Reading Tool

Explanation:

This reading tool is a great help for young children because it focuses attention on a small amount of text at one time. It can also be beneficial to some older students who may still experience difficulty with eye tracking and keeping their place when reading.

From A HISTORY OF US: WAR, PEACE, AND ALL THAT JAZZ (VOL 9) by Joy Hakim, © 1995 by Joy Hakim. Used by permission of Oxford University Press, Inc.

Materials:

- Reading Tool (see pattern, page 126)
- Tagboard
- Sheets of glossy colored acetate
- Glue or double-sided permanent tape

Directions:

1. To make your own reading tool, cut a 7x2-inch strip from the tagboard and a 7x1-inch strip from the colored acetate. Using either glue or double-sided permanent tape, attach the acetate to the tagboard so that about ½ inch extends beyond the tagboard.

2. Have the student position the reading tool on the text so that the colored strip is on the bottom of the tagboard, highlighting just one or two lines of text. Placing it this way allows the eyes to make a return sweep down to the next line.

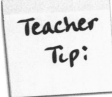
Teacher Tip:

1. In addition to using glossy colored acetate, have students try frosted acetate, experimenting to see which side of the frosted type works better for each individual.

Colored Overlays to Bring Print into Focus

Textbook Talk-back Notes

Explanation:

When students with Irlen Syndrome/Scotopic Sensitivity read black print on white paper, the words may appear to shake, letters may seem to rotate, and the print may seem out of focus. It has been found that by placing either frosted or glossy colored overlays over the print, visual distortions are dramatically reduced.

Materials:

- Frosted or glossy overlays of various colors (see page 149)

Colored overlay

From *A HISTORY OF US: WAR, PEACE, AND ALL THAT JAZZ (VOL 9) by Joy Hakim, © 1995 by Joy Hakim. Used by permission of Oxford University Press, Inc.*

Directions:

1. Provide overlays of different colors to your students and allow each one to experiment with the colors to discover which works best for him/her.

2. Have students try both frosted and glossy types; also have them see if one or the other side of the frosted overlay has a more noticeable effect.

Teacher Tips:

1. Try the Self-Test for Irlen Syndrome/Scotopic Sensitivity (see page 127).

Adapted with permission from Reading by the Colors *by Helen L. Irlen, Penguin Putnam/Perigee Div. Publishers.*

Post-it Notes and Codes

Explanation:

This active-reading strategy helps students focus as they read, quickly identify important information, and make a connection to the text. It also provides you with concrete evidence of what students do or do not understand as well as visible proof of their efforts to read and comprehend.

Materials:

- Post-it notes, or similar products, in a variety of shapes, sizes, and colors

Directions:

1. Provide students with a variety of Post-it notes, or similar products, and set a purpose for reading. (This means students think ahead about what they are going to get out of their reading. For example, are they going to be informed or entertained?)

2. Instruct students to use the notes (especially the arrow-shaped type) to point out important information that they will want to review again in the future.

3. Have students "code" the text as they read, and decide with them what codes to use. For example, an exclamation mark (!) could mean "This is interesting." A question mark (?) could mean "I don't understand this." An asterisk (*) could mean "I already know this."

4. Ask them to write the appropriate codes on a number of Post-it notes, marking one code per note.

5. Have them read the textbook chapter and, while reading, use the notes to code the text each time they come to an interesting fact, a text-to-text connection, or whatever they are coding for.

6. Encourage students to write quick-review notes on their Post-its. These could be about important people, places, events, and/or terminology.

Textbook Talk-back
Notes

Teacher Tips:

1. Decide ahead of time what your students will be coding for and what codes to use.

2. After reading and coding the text, have students use the Read-Pair-Share strategy (see page 71) for a Post-it note discussion.

3. Be sure to have an adequate supply of Post-it notes on hand for each student. Transparent ones are great for highlighting important text.

4. Encourage students to save and reuse any notes that have not been written on.

5. Suggest that they transfer their quick-review notes to blank notebook paper for future chapter reviews.

Using a Focus Frame

Explanation:

This easy-to-make tool helps students slide words, sentences, or math problems into focus, eliminating other potentially distracting text or pictures from the student's view. In math, it allows a student to do one step at a time and minimizes the chance for errors.

Materials:

- Manila folder, poster board, tagboard, or other heavy-stock paper

Directions:

1. Using the pattern that is provided (see page 128), cut out the two pieces—A and B. Or, to keep this pattern page intact, photocopy the page and cut out the two pieces from the copied page. Trace around pieces A and B on the material of choice (poster board, tagboard, etc.) and cut out the pieces.

2. Cut two long slits in piece A, as shown in the example.

3. Insert one end of piece B into a slit on A, and the other end of B into the other slit on A. Now you have a movable box that can be enlarged or reduced in size. You will be able to focus on words and sentences as well as math problems. If working on a math addition problem, show students how they can begin with the units and then slide to the tens column, the hundreds, etc.

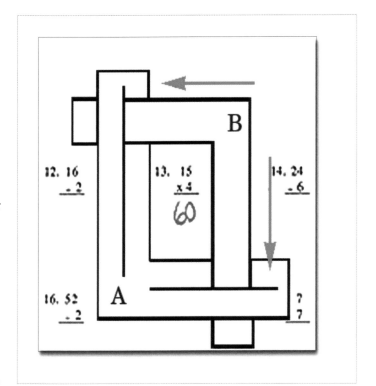

Teacher Tips:

1. Allow students to keep these Focus Frames at their desks to use during daily work and testing when appropriate.

2. Have students make these in a variety of sizes. They can put their names on their frames to stay focused on organization too!

Active Bookmarks

INDIVIDUAL   SMALL GROUP
PAIRS   WHOLE GROUP

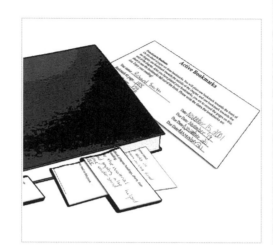

Explanation:

This nonthreatening strategy engages students during reading and keeps them focused on the textbook content.

Materials:

- Active Bookmarks reproducible (see page 129)

Directions:

1. Give each student an Active Bookmark sheet with due dates filled in.

2. Have students follow the directions on the sheet:

   a. Cut apart the bookmarks.

   b. Randomly open the textbook and place the bookmarks throughout the pages of the chapter. For example, put the first one toward the front of the chapter, the second toward the middle, and the third toward the end of the chapter.

   c. Record the page where each bookmark is located and the due date for it.

3. During the reading of the textbook chapter, when a student comes to the page where a bookmark is located, he or she completes the assignment on the bookmark and turns it in at the appropriate time.

Teacher Tips:

1. Prepare the bookmark sheet in advance.

2. As a follow-up activity, have your students share their bookmarks in small groups.

3. Your students' bookmarks could all be on different pages since each student randomly opens his/her book in the front, middle, and end of the chapter you specify.

Textbook Talk-back Notes

Eliminate Transferring Time and Copying Errors

INDIVIDUAL   SMALL GROUP
PAIRS   WHOLE GROUP

Explanation:

This strategy will help increase the productivity of math students who work at a slower pace or who would otherwise make careless mistakes copying problems from the book onto their papers.

Materials:

- Sheets of acetate
- Paper clips or nonpermanent tape
- Dry-erase or water-soluble marker

Directions:

1. Attach a sheet of acetate to the math book page, using paper clips or nonpermanent tape.

2. Have the student write the answer to the problem on this sheet, using a dry-erase or water-soluble marker.

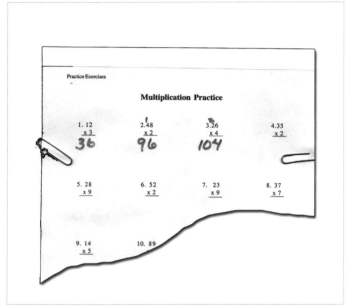

Teacher Tips:

1. A plastic page protector cut down to the size of the book and placed over the page may work well enough so that paper clips or tape is not needed. Be sure to leave one corner or side of the plastic page protector intact so it won't slip off.

2. Give your discouraged students only one page at a time.

3. Another alternative for reducing copying errors is to make an enlarged photocopy of the math textbook page on an 11x17-inch sheet of paper. This provides more work space for computing. You might also wish to eliminate any distracting artwork as you make the copies. Always secure permission first from the textbook publisher before making copies of any material under copyright. (See page 113 for a permission form you could use for this purpose.)

Drawing the Words

INDIVIDUAL	SMALL GROUP
PAIRS	WHOLE GROUP

Textbook Talk-back Notes

Explanation:

One of the keys to improving comprehension is getting students to visualize what they are reading. Your goal is to have them read the words, then close their eyes and try to visualize what they just read, then draw a simple image of what they imagined.

Materials:

- Large sheets of paper
- Markers

Directions:

1. Have students provide illustrations for the following types of text:

   a. Math word problems

   b. Step-by-step procedures in science (a sketch for each step)

   c. Paragraphs of expository text. (These drawings may vary a great deal in subject matter, depending on what image the text conjured up for each student.)

2. Remind your students that stick figures are fine to use—each student is just giving you a sketch of what you hope is a more elaborate image in his/her head!

1. Make overhead transparency copies of the students' paragraph drawings. Reduce them if necessary so you can cut them up and show three or four images at the same time on the overhead. Use these images to stimulate a class discussion about how individuals imagine the text differently depending on their own prior knowledge. (If my only knowledge of a boat is the family rowboat, then that's probably what George Washington is going to be in when he crosses the Delaware.)

2. Use these transparencies (one transparency for each text paragraph) to have the whole class or a small group of students try to sequence them in the same order as the text.

Recorded Textbooks

INDIVIDUAL PAIRS   SMALL GROUP WHOLE GROUP

Explanation:

Recorded textbooks can be engaging and can help students with reading difficulties boost their listening comprehension while building an "I can read" attitude. This is a great way to narrow the achievement gap by scaffolding reading instruction with auditory support for slow or struggling readers.

Materials:

- Audiocassette recordings of text chapters or assigned sections
- Audiocassette players with or without headphones

Directions:

1. Record individual chapters and/or nightly reading assignments from the textbook for students to use individually, in pairs, or in small groups.

2. Direct students to read along in their textbooks as they are listening to the recordings.

3. Suggest that students use headphones to listen to the books on tape during transitional times, such as when they are waiting for or riding the school bus or are waiting for an after-school activity to begin.

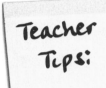

1. Secure permission from the textbook publisher before recording copyrighted material (see permission form, page 113).

2. Ask for student or adult volunteers to assist you in recording the textbook material.

3. Take advantage of prerecorded textbooks (see pages 149-150).

Noise-Suppressing Headphones for Concentrating

Textbook Talk-back Notes

Explanation:

By eliminating outside noises, noise-suppressing headphones help students who are sensitive to auditory distractions concentrate on their reading. These headphones come in handy at times other than reading, too.

Materials:

- Noise-suppressing headphones

Directions:

1. Purchase noise-suppressing headphones, available at most hardware stores.

2. Provide them to students when they are engaged in work that requires a great deal of concentration, as they block out extraneous sounds that can take students off task.

Teacher Tip:

1. Avoid stigmatizing students by encouraging others to use the headphones, thus popularizing this accommodation.

Power Thinking

Explanation:

This strategy helps students take notes as they actively read the textbook, classify information, and understand main ideas and details. In Power Thinking, each concept gets a power number. The power 1s are the main ideas, the power 2s are the details for the power 1s, the power 3s are the details for the power 2s, and so on. It is important that the powers keep the same relationship to one another. Students learn to apply power thinking as they read their textbooks in order to help sort main ideas from details.

Materials:

- Index cards

Directions:

1. Start teaching Power Thinking by modeling the strategy and using categories that are familiar to your students. One example of Power Thinking might look like this:

   Power 1. Sports

           Power 2. Football

               Power 3. Bills

               Power 3. Cowboys

           Power 2. Baseball

               Power 3. Cardinals

               Power 3. Giants

               Power 3. Astros

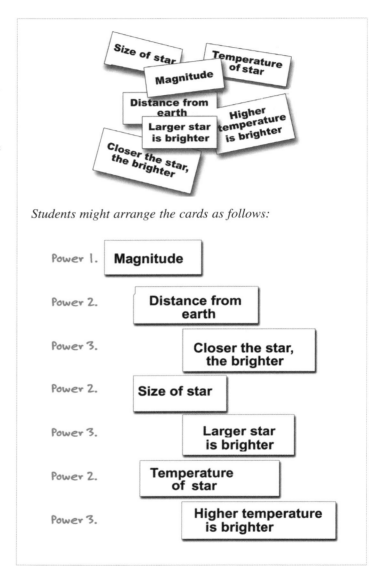

Students might arrange the cards as follows:

Power 1. **Magnitude**

Power 2. **Distance from earth**

Power 3. **Closer the star, the brighter**

Power 2. **Size of star**

Power 3. **Larger star is brighter**

Power 2. **Temperature of star**

Power 3. **Higher temperature is brighter**

2. Ask your students to practice Power Thinking using material from their text-books. Put a variety of Power 1, 2, and 3 terms on index cards—one term per card but without the power number. Give the cards to a small group of students. Ask them to figure out what power each term represents and then to arrange the cards to reflect their Power Thinking. For example, cards for a textbook chapter on "Characteristics of Stars" might be: Higher temperature is brighter; Distance from earth; Magnitude; Temperature of star; Larger star is brighter; Closer the star, the brighter; Size of star.

Students might arrange the cards as follows:

Power 1. Magnitude

Power 2. Distance from earth

Power 3. Closer the star, the brighter

Power 2. Size of star

Power 3. Larger star is brighter

Power 2. Temperature of star

Power 3. Higher temperature is brighter

You want students involved in active discussions as they manipulate and arrange the cards in order.

Teacher Tip:

1. Read the textbook material ahead of time and model Power Thinking for a section from the book in order to guide the students in this technique.

Content Puzzles

Explanation:

Content Puzzles help students take notes and re-member information. They also provide a way for them to distinguish between key concepts and subordi-nate ideas in the textbook. The puzzle headings pro-vide students with a focus for reading.

Materials:

- Content Puzzle graphic organizer (see page 130)

Directions:

1. Before your students start reading in depth, ask them to skim the textbook chapter and make a list of important ideas or topics.

2. Have them write each topic as a heading on one of the puzzle pieces of the graphic organizer. For example, if the reading is about silkworms, the headings might be "Description," "Food," "Homes," "Stages of Develop-ment," and "Interesting Facts."

3. As students are reading, they write on the puzzle piece the words or phrases from the textbook chapter that fit into each category.

4. Process what students have done through a class discussion so they can understand the important concepts in each category.

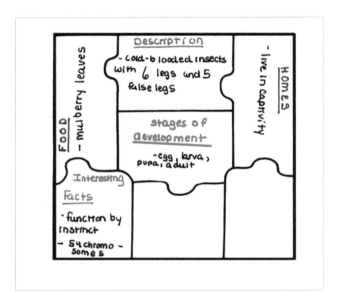

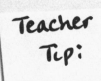

Teacher Tip:

1. Identify the important ideas ahead of time yourself and place the headings in the puzzle pieces for the students.

Note Taking with Graphic Organizers

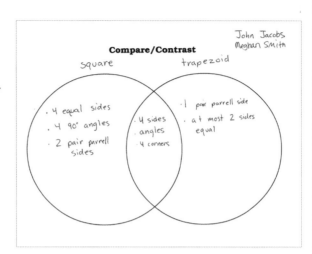

Textbook Talk-back Notes

Explanation:

This strategy utilizes graphic organizers as note-taking devices that can be matched to the text structure of the textbook chapter that the students are reading. For example, if their textbook is comparing/contrasting squares and trapezoids, the Venn Diagram graphic organizer could be used. This helps students organize their thinking and visualize the connections among the ideas presented in the chapter.

Materials:

- Graphic organizer reproducibles (see pages 131-135)

Directions:

1. Ask students to use pointer/signal words identified during their pre-reading of the chapter (see Pointer/Signal Words and Text Structure, page 52) to determine the type of text structure in which they think the text is written.

2. Model for your students how to use graphic organizers to take notes while reading.

3. Have students hypothesize which of the five graphic organizers would be the best to use to take notes while they are reading the textbook chapter.

4. Ask them to read the text silently, using their graphic organizers to take notes.

5. Once they are familiar with this strategy, have your students create their own graphic organizers to help them as they read and take notes.

Teacher Tips:

1. Remember that not all texts fit just one particular text structure, and sometimes you may need to create a new graphic organizer other than the five we have provided, or guide your students as they create one for themselves.

2. Give the students graphic organizers that are partly filled in (the cloze procedure) as a way to support them as they read the text and take notes.

Textbook Talk-back Notes

Explanation:

Learning and comprehension can improve when students are actively involved with reading materials. With Textbook Talk-back Notes students make notes in their own words, which results in a more personal connection to the text.

Materials:

- Textbook Talk-back Notes reproducible (see page 136)
- Nonpermanent tape

Directions:

1. Provide enough copies of the Textbook Talk-back Notes so each student will have one for each page of his/her reading.

2. Have students attach a note strip in the margin of each textbook page using nonpermanent tape.

3. Encourage students to think aloud and to write their thoughts or questions concerning the text on the note strips as they read each page.

4. Have students save these notes so they can review them while answering their homework questions on the material.

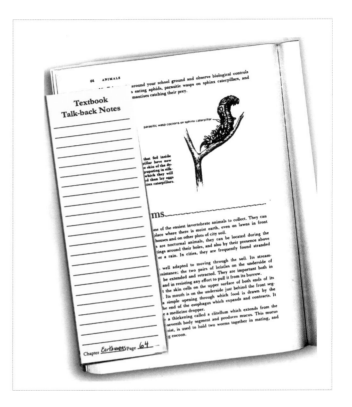

Teacher Tips:

1. When students finish each chapter, have each staple his/her Textbook Talk-back Notes together so they can be used later when reviewing for exams.

2. Give left-handed students the option of taping their strips to the margin on the left side of the page.

Reprinted with permission from Ten-Minute Field Trips, *Third Edition, Revised, © 2001, by NSTA Press, National Science Teachers Association.*

Read-Pair-Share

INDIVIDUAL   SMALL GROUP
PAIRS   **WHOLE GROUP**

Textbook Talk-back
Notes

Explanation:

Some students need support as they are reading the textbook. This strategy provides opportunities for them to talk about the text with classmates as they are reading it.

Directions:

1. Group students into pairs.

2. Point out appropriate places for students to stop when they read the textbook and ask them to mark those places with pieces of paper or Post-it notes.

3. Have students read individually to the first stopping point and ask them to code the text using the Post-it Notes and Codes strategy (see page 58) as they read.

4. After they have completed the reading, have the paired students talk with one another, using their Post-it notes to remind them of the points each wishes to discuss.

5. Have the whole class share the interesting points that arose during their paired discussions.

6. When the first Read-Pair-Share cycle has been completed, have students read the next portion of the text and repeat what they did the first time, with either a new partner or the same one.

Teacher Tips:

1. See Chapter 1 for quick and easy ways to group students into pairs.

2. Identify stopping points for discussions of the textbook material ahead of time.

3. Ask your students to share words they didn't know or facts that surprised them.

Three-Step Interview

Explanation:

This activity involves three students working together and rotating the roles of interviewer, interviewee, and recorder. For example, in science, students might be reading a chapter on plants that includes a section on photosynthesis. Students stop and summarize what they read through the interview process. After each paragraph or section, they rotate roles.

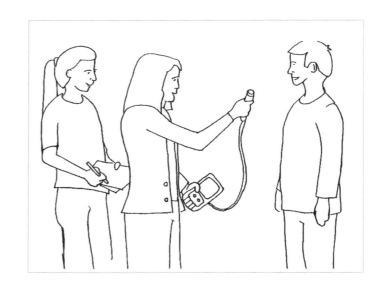

Materials:

- Writing paper or a journal
- Microphone and tape recorder (optional)
- Videotape recorder (optional)

Directions:

1. Decide what sections of the text you would like students to read and indicate at what points in the text they will stop to do the three-step interview.

2. Assign students to work in groups of three: one student conducts the interview (perhaps with a microphone and tape recorder), one is interviewed, and one records the interview on paper (or with a video recorder).

3. Students continue this process through the reading assignment, rotating among the three roles. As one student conducts the interview, the recorder can also write down questions or points of clarification the group might like to raise at the end of the session.

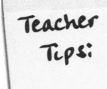
Teacher Tips:

1. Prior to class, mark or designate the text that you want to be read and where students should stop to conduct interviews.

2. Before using this procedure with the textbook, model and practice the three-step interview on a familiar topic, such as: What do you most like to do on weekends?

3. Refer to Chapter 1 for quick and easy ways to group students, or let them group themselves.

Personal Learning Timelines

INDIVIDUAL   *SMALL GROUP*
PAIRS   **WHOLE GROUP**

Explanation:

Personal Learning Timelines enable students to remain actively engaged in their reading while gaining a better understanding of the text. This strategy works well with historical topics such as the Civil War; with areas of science such as the different plants and animals that lived during specific periods of earth's history; with current events, social studies, etc. When students keep timelines, it helps them focus on names and dates of important events and allows them to make connections.

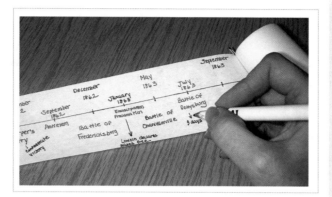

Materials:

• Adding machine tape

Directions:

1. Show your students examples of timelines from published books.

2. Over the course of a few lessons, model a timeline on the overhead projector. Create the timeline with the class as you study a segment from the textbook.

3. Give each student a roll of adding machine tape. Explain that students can record important details and dates as they read, creating their own individual timelines for study purposes.

Teacher Tips:

1. Students can also use the timeline as a novel way to journal at the end of a class or end of a day. Students reflect on important learning, then record or illustrate it on their personal learning timelines. They write the current date and then add examples of what they learned, ranging from vocabulary words to types of math problems solved. Throughout the year, students can roll out their learning timelines to see the progress they have made.

2. To prevent the adding machine tapes from getting tangled, torn, or in some other state of disrepair, have your students store them rolled up and secured with rubber bands or paper clips.

Textbook Talk-back Notes

Math Word Problem Graphic Organizer

INDIVIDUAL   SMALL GROUP
PAIRS   WHOLE GROUP

Explanation:

Words can get in the way of the math required to solve a word problem, so it is helpful to break the problem-solving process into manageable steps. Using a graphic organizer, students can make better sense of the question being asked and the information needed to solve the problem. Once they have identified these important details, students can continue to solve the problem and check their answers for reasonableness.

Materials:

- Math Word Problem Graphic Organizer (see page 137)

Directions:

1. Copy the graphic organizer and give one copy to each student.

2. Help students take a step-by-step approach to solving word problems. Begin by having them read the problem first, then show them how to rewrite it in their own words on their graphic organizers in the question mark section.

3. Help students identify the facts needed to solve the problem and demonstrate how to transfer this information to the magnifying-glass section of their graphic organizers.

4. Work with students as they write an equation and solve the problem.

5. In the "thumbs up" section, model how to check to be sure the answer is reasonable.

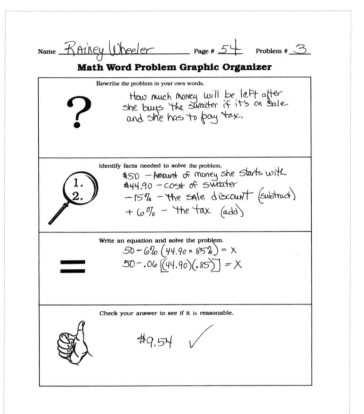

Teacher Tips:

1. When teaching students to solve word problems, start with a few easy ones to help them internalize the process.

2. For students who have strong auditory skills but struggle with reading, provide a tape recorder. Encourage them to rephrase the questions and to explain the reasonableness of their answers on tape.

Mind-Mapping for Understanding

Textbook Talk-back Notes

Explanation:

A mind map is a way to use symbols, pictures, colors, etc., to create a nonlinguistic representation of text. Mind-mapping is a highly effective visualization activity for students to use to organize their thoughts, take meaningful notes, and make text connections as they read. Later, these maps can serve as helpful study guides before a test.

Mind map for Water States & Cycle

Materials:

- Paper
- Colored pencils or markers

Directions:

1. Model this strategy first with a simple subject to familiarize students with the procedure.

2. Give students a topic or central idea to map and tell them to write it in the center of their maps. From this main idea, major themes will branch out, each containing related key images or words.

3. Have students identify what these major themes are, thus helping reinforce text connections in their own minds.

Teacher Tips:

1. Make overheads of different examples of mind maps to help students see how they work, as well as how each one is unique to the individual learner.

2. Have small groups create a collaborative mind map.

3. Encourage students to use color with their mind maps to make the information more memorable.

Hearing the Text: Onomatopoeia

INDIVIDUAL PAIRS SMALL GROUP WHOLE GROUP

Explanation:

To increase your students' visualization of the setting or event that is being described in their textbook, have them try to "hear" what they have read.

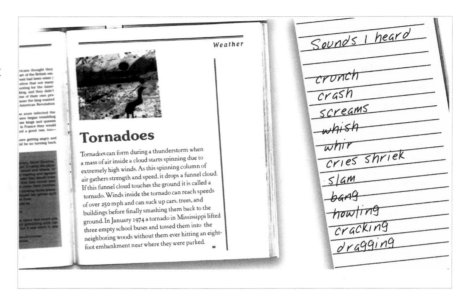

Directions:

1. Have a class discussion about the meaning of the word "onomatopoeia," starting with its definition in the dictionary: the naming of a thing or action by a vocal imitation of the sound associated with it, such as "buzz" or "hiss."

2. Share a few sound words with your students and ask them to come up with others.

3. Read a paragraph from the text. When you are finished, ask the students to imagine they were putting background sounds to your reading—as if they were working on a radio or television program or on a movie. Discuss some of the choices they come up with. Depending on their prior knowledge, the "sounds" they hear could vary a great deal.

4. Have the students continue to work on their own, writing sound words that they "hear" after they read different sections of the text.

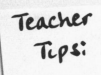

Teacher Tips:

1. Choose a letter of the alphabet and see how many sound words beginning with that letter your students can write in one minute.

2. Practicing using sound words will, it is hoped, cross over to make student writing come alive and be more interesting.

After-Reading Strategies

During this phase, students must integrate the information from the textbook into what they already know about the topic. The emphasis now is on keeping your students motivated to learn and enhancing their understanding of what they have read. This chapter includes a wide range of individual as well as collaborative learning activities that help students organize, categorize, and analyze content material; write summaries of the information; process and review the material in novel ways; and respond to the textbook questions.

Inside/Outside Review Circles

INDIVIDUAL **SMALL GROUP**
PAIRS WHOLE GROUP

Explanation:

This cooperative learning structure provides opportunities for students to respond to textbook questions in a novel manner. With students grouped into inside and outside circles, they take turns asking and responding to textbook or teacher-generated questions. By rotating the outer circle, each student has the opportunity to work with more than one partner.

Materials:

- Signal for students to rotate (bell, chimes, train whistle, music, etc.)

Outside circle moves clockwise

Directions:

1. Decide what review questions or topic needs to be addressed in the group.

2. Arrange students in even-numbered groups, with a minimum of six per group.

3. Divide each group in half: one half forms an inside circle with the students facing out, the other half forms an outside circle with the students facing in and standing opposite someone in the inside circle. (In cases of odd numbers of students, place two together in the outside circle and have them take turns.)

4. Explain which circle will ask the questions and which circle will respond. (No one writes anything down.)

5. Announce group guidelines:

   - Respectful Rules/No Put Downs

   - Response Time

   - Rotation Direction

6. Use a signal to begin and then monitor the responses being given.

7. After a set time, signal the outside circle to rotate clockwise so that each child stands in front of a new student.

Teacher Tip:

1. Model, then practice the rules, response time, and rotation before actually using this strategy.

Give All or Part of the Answer

Textbook Talk-back
Notes

Explanation:

Giving students letter-clues to questions on homework provides them with a little extra support to help them narrow their field of answer choices. This is similar to solving a crossword puzzle when you know how many letters there are in your answer.

Directions:

1. For fill-in-the-blank questions, give different types of clues to help students figure out the answers.

2. For example, you could provide the first letter of the word that is the answer. Or you might include a space for each letter of the word and fill in the last letter as well. Or you could simply include a space for each letter of the word that answers the question.

1. C_____

(first letter of the answer is capital "C")

2. _ _ _ _ r

(five-letter answer ending in "r")

3. _ _ _ _ _ _ _

(seven-letter answer)

Teacher
Tip:

1. For multi-step math problems, give them the final answer! This not only provides students with a twist on solving problems but also conveys a message that the procedure is as important as the answer.

Crossword Puzzles:
Standard, Backward, and In-between

Explanation:

Crossword puzzles provide a challenging yet entertaining way to introduce and reinforce the meanings of new words and terminology. Varying the approach you take to providing clues also helps to keep students motivated.

Directions:

1. Decide on the words, terms, names, etc. you want to review from the textbook and write them down.

2. Once you have decided on how to arrange them in crossword-puzzle fashion, create a crossword grid.

3. Write consecutive numbers in the squares where the horizontally placed words and the vertically placed words should go.

4. Write the corresponding number clues for across words and down words as there are horizontal and vertical squares.

5. Decide on the approach you want to take before completing the copy master for the students:

   a. Standard Crossword—You give the students the clues or definitions and they fill in the puzzle's squares.

   b. Backward Crossword—You fill in the squares with the words and they write the definitions.

   c. In-between Crossword—You combine the two above, providing some words and some clues.

6. Complete the copy master and make a copy for each student.

Wolves

Across:

1. Year the government stopped paying hunters to kill wolves.

2. Name given to a group of wolves who travel and live together.

4. _____

7. National Park used to relocate wolves to when they were identified as endangered.

8. _____

12. Name of second-ranking male or female wolf.

Down:

1. Year the Endangered Species Act was passed.

3. Name given to dominate male and female wolf.

4. Name of young wolf.

5. _____

6. An animal that hunts other animals.

9. _____

10. _____

11. An animal who is hunted by another animal.

An in-between crossword puzzle

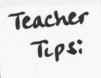

Teacher Tips:

1. Let students decide for themselves which approach they want to take in creating their crossword puzzles.

2. Go online to check out some of the web sites pertaining to crossword puzzles (see page 152). There are many of them and some may inspire additional ideas regarding this activity.

Information Grid:
Organizing, Categorizing, and Analyzing

Textbook Talk-back Notes

Explanation:

This strategy helps students think about the similarities and differences among concepts in the textbook. It provides a unique framework for organizing and categorizing textbook information and helps students synthesize information and take notes while reading.

Category: Insect Orders

Features

INSECT ORDERS	Two pairs of wings	Molt throughout adult life	Forceps on abdomen	Powerful forelegs
Coleoptera	+	–	–	?
Collembola	+	+	–	?
Dermaptera	–	+	+	–

Members

Symbols:
+ = yes
— = no
? = don't know

Materials:

- Organizing, Categorizing, and Analyzing Grid reproducible (see page 138)

Directions:

1. From the textbook that students have read, choose a category to use for the grid, such as Insect Orders. At the top of the far left-hand column of the grid, write "Insect Orders" and then list vertically under it some of the members of this category, such as "Coleoptera," "Collembola," and "Dermaptera." Moving horizontally across the top of the grid, list the features of this category (Insect Orders), such as "Two pairs of wings," "Molt throughout adult life," "Forceps on abdomen," and "Powerful forelegs."

2. Use plus and minus symbols as an easy way for students to indicate their answers. For example, a plus (+) sign could mean the insect order has the feature listed, a minus (-) sign could mean it does not have the feature, and a question mark (?) could indicate that the student is not sure.

Teacher Tips:

1. Let the students use completed charts, which have been checked and corrected, if necessary, for later review and study.

2. An overabundance of question marks is probably an indicator of a student's fear of predicting because he/she doesn't want to write the wrong answer. You may, therefore, want to eliminate that mark as a choice.

Leveling Questions

Explanation:

This strategy uses the question-answer relationship as a basis for leveling different types of questions. A good working vocabulary to use with students is "Level I: Right There," "Level II: Search and Find," "Level III: Author and Me." and "Level IV: On My Own." It is easier for struggling students in particular to understand these terms rather than the words "literal" or "inferential." Leveling questions helps students skim textbook material to look for answers and makes them better question writers too.

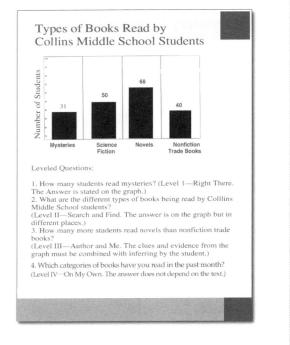

Types of Books Read by Collins Middle School Students

Leveled Questions:

1. How many students read mysteries? (Level 1—Right There. The Answer is stated on the graph.)
2. What are the different types of books being read by Colllins Middle School students?
(Level II—Search and Find. The answer is on the graph but in different places.)
3. How many more students read novels than nonfiction trade books?
(Level III—Author and Me. The clues and evidence from the graph must be combined with inferring by the student.)

4. Which categories of books have you read in the past month?
(Level IV—On My Own. The answer does not depend on the text.)

Directions:

1. Begin by teaching your students the four levels of questions. (It is helpful to start out using low-level content first, as in the example that follows about *Goldilocks and the Three Bears.*)

   a. Level I: Right There (In the Book)—The answer is stated in the text. Example from *Goldilocks and the Three Bears*: "What did Mama Bear pour in the bowls?" Tell students that many times, the words in a Level I question are repeated in the answer. "Mama Bear poured mush in the bowls." This is really "reading the lines."

   b. Level II: Search and Find (In the Book)—The answer is stated in the text but it is more difficult to locate. Example: "Where did Goldilocks go in the bears' house?" Level II questions require students to use different pieces of information right from the textbook to figure out the answer. Unlike the Level I question, the answer to a Level II question is not found in just one place in the textbook. Students would need to look in several places in the text to find the answer.

   c. Level III: Author and Me (In my Head)—The answer to this level of question is not stated in the text; clues and evidence are given so the text still needs to be read. Example: "How did Goldilocks probably feel when she saw the three bears?" Emphasize to students that they must look for clues and evidence from the author and then combine it with what is in their own heads (prior knowledge) to correctly answer Level III questions.

   d. Level IV: On My Own (In My Head)—The answer is not dependent on the text. Rather the answer comes from the student's prior knowledge. For example, "Have you ever known that someone else has been in your bedroom at home? How did you know?" You have a reason for teaching this last category, even though it relies on prior knowledge and not on the text. If you don't teach students the different types of questions, then they sometimes tend to answer everything as if it were an On-My-Own question. Teach this category so you can point out these things to students later.

2. Use picture books and/or low-level content to teach students to distinguish different levels of questions. Model this thoroughly for your students. Tell them that the first step in correctly answering a question is to be able to identify the type of question that it is.

3. After students can identify the four different levels of questions, divide them into groups.

4. Ask students to look at the questions in their textbooks and see if they can level the questions. Make certain each group justifies its decisions. It is the thinking and the discussion that you are after.

5. Challenge groups of students to write Level I, II, III, and IV questions from low-level content such as picture books and then to write questions from their textbook reading.

6. Have other students try to guess what level each question is. Again, you are after the thinking process and the interaction of students with the text.

Teacher Tips:

1. Use leveled questions for math word problems, too.

    a. Level I (Right There/In the Word Problem): If Sarah has five marbles and Tim has three, how many more marbles does Sarah have than Tim?

    b. Level II (Search and Find/In the Word Problem): During the summer, Heather earned $35 baby-sitting and $28 weeding the family garden. She would like to buy a pair of shoes on sale for $23, plus attend a concert with a ticket price of $40. Will she have enough money to do both? How much extra does she have or how much more will she need?

    c. Level III (Math and Me/In My Head): Sue and Drew are sisters. Sue is 3 years old and Drew is 5. How old will both girls be when the sum of the digits in both their ages is 8 again? In this type of problem, students must stop and consider the problem-solving strategies they have learned to logically solve the problem.

    d. Level IV (On My Own/In My Head): Create your own word problem, involving at least 2 steps and 3 operations.

Potluck Reading

INDIVIDUAL   **SMALL GROUP**
PAIRS   WHOLE GROUP

Explanation:

Potluck Reading accommodates a wide range of reading abilities in a content area. The strategy also allows students the opportunity to learn from one another as well as practice summarizing information from the textbook.

Directions:

1. Arrange students in groups of three to four individuals.

2. Give each group member a different section of the textbook chapter to read.

3. Have each student read his/her section independently, taking notes to record important information.

4. Regroup students who read the same passage into "expert groups." Have these experts compare their notes and come up with a consensus of the main points in their section of the textbook.

5. Ask students to return to their original groups and share the pertinent information from their sections of the text. Each group member is responsible for taking notes on every other member's presentation so that all students are accountable for all the material in the textbook chapter.

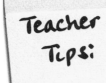

Teacher Tips:

1. Select reading passages ahead of time.

2. Refer to Chapter 1 for quick and easy ways to group students, or let them form their own groups.

3. Eventually let each student choose for him/herself the section of the textbook chapter to read.

Transforming Information in the Text

Textbook Talk-back Notes

Explanation:

This is an effective way to get information from the text into your students' long-term memories. When they recast the information (print) into another medium (drawing/ graphic), their understanding of the concepts presented in the textbook is enhanced.

Materials:

- Large sheets of paper
- Markers

Directions:

1. Divide students into small groups and give each group a large sheet of paper and a supply of markers.

2. After your students read a section of the textbook, ask each group to decide what the most important information in the passage is and then devise a way to show it graphically on their sheet of paper. Tell them that there is no one correct way to create their drawing or graphic. The only requirement is that it show their understanding of the relationships within the textbook material they have read.

3. Encourage them to use color, pictures, symbols, and only a few words when creating their graphic.

4. Have each group present their creation to the rest of the class.

Teacher Tips:

1. Before asking your students to do this, model how you would make a picture or graphic so they can see what a finished product might look like.

2. Hang up completed projects in the classroom.

R.A.F.T.

Explanation:

This strategy provides writing practice at the same time that it helps students process information. Students consolidate what they have learned from the textbook and then write from a viewpoint other than their own to an audience other than the teacher and in a format other than answering questions at the end of the textbook chapter. R.A.F.T. is an acronym that stands for:

R =   **Role of the writer**
A =   **Audience for the writer**
F =   **Format of the writing**
T =   **Topic of the writing**

Directions:

1. Talk with students about the important points in a textbook passage they have read and brainstorm the different roles the writer and audience could have, and what the writing format and topic could be for the R.A.F.T. assignment.

2. Tell the students to include factual material in their written pieces.

1. Extend the activity by having students pair up and exchange notes. Each can then write a response to the original letter, giving another point of view.

Textbook Pictionary

Explanation:

Content-area teachers can use this strategy to incorporate vocabulary work into their instruction. It activates student involvement and is a novel and fun alternative to simply looking up terms in a dictionary.

Materials:

- Index cards
- Flip chart with large paper or a white board
- Timer

Directions:

1. Provide students with a list and a brief definition of the content-area concepts or words they should know from the textbook chapter they are studying.

2. Write each term on an index card, including only one per card.

3. Divide your class into two groups.

4. Have one student from one of the groups come to the front of the room where you have a flip chart or white board set up.

5. Give the student one of the index cards and then, after setting a timer for 2 to 3 minutes, signal him or her to start drawing a picture (or pictures) that gives clues to the word on the card.

6. The rest of the students consult their sheets with all the words and definitions on it. The group that the student up front is from tries to guess what the word is. If they guess correctly within the allotted time, that group wins a point.

7. Next, have a student from the second group go to the flow chart, give him/her an index card, and follow the same procedure described above. Repeat until each student has had a turn. The group with the most correct answers wins.

8. Gather up the pictures, and the next day show one of them to your class and ask them to pronounce and define the word.

Teacher Tips:

1. Prepare in advance the list of words and definitions as well as the set of index cards with the words written on them.

2. If you don't have a flip chart or easel in your classroom, simply attach a sheet of 11x17-inch paper to the blackboard with masking tape and have the student draw on that. Take it down after each turn and replace with a clean sheet.

3. A fun alternative is to turn this into the game of Charades and have the students act out the words on their cards instead of drawing them.

Textbook Talk-back Notes

Three Facts and a Fib

Explanation:

This activity gives students a chance to review and process content from the text in a fun, interactive way. It is important to model and practice this first. Students sometimes find it hard to remember that what they want to do is fool or trick as many other students as they can with their false statements.

Materials:

- Index cards

Directions:

1. After your students read an assigned textbook section, ask each of them to think of four statements about the content. Three should be true and one should be false.

2. Have the students write each statement on a separate index card. For example, if the subject is geometry solids, a student's statements might be as follows:

   a. A dodecahedron has 10 faces.

   b. A cube has 6 faces.

   c. An octahedron has 8 faces.

   d. An icosahedron has 20 faces.

3. Have the students circulate around the classroom, show their index cards to one another, and try to identify the "fibs."

4. If a student cannot guess another classmate's fib, he/she must sign or initial one of that student's index cards; the student who has the most signatures (who has fooled the most classmates) wins the game.

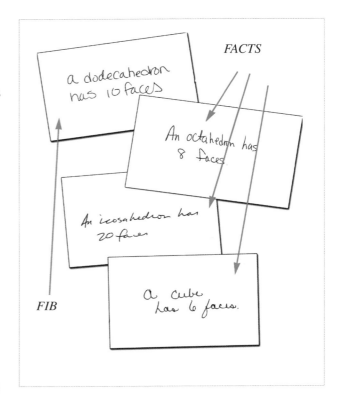

1. Be sure to practice this with your students using something familiar. Remind them that if they cannot guess which of the statements is the fib, then you have tricked them, so they must sign their name to your paper. And that's what the students who do not guess the fib correctly have to do—sign the paper of the student who fooled or tricked them.

Taped Responses

Textbook Talk-back Notes

Explanation:

Some students have a great deal of difficulty distilling information and getting their thoughts down on paper even though they know the answers to the textbook questions. It may be that their oral and auditory language skills are stronger than their written skills. If this is the case, taping their responses will be especially beneficial to them.

The three steps involved in this strategy will help build up confidence and level the playing field for struggling learners.

Materials:

- Cassette recorder
- Ten-minute tapes (see page 150)

Directions:

1. Have the student read the questions and then formulate the answers in his/her head.

2. Provide the student with a cassette recorder and ten-minute tape and ask him/her to record the answers.

3. Have the student replay the tape and transcribe his/her answers.

Teacher Tip:

1. Using shorter, ten-minute tapes is a time-saver for students who might have difficulty finding their responses on tapes of longer duration.

Text Souvenirs

Explanation:

Many of us purchase or find souvenirs to remind us of places we have visited, and this activity draws from a similar idea. Ask your students to create and/or find souvenirs of their learning and keep them in a special souvenir or memory box. It's a good way to review textbook content, as students pull out souvenirs and reflect on their meaning.

Materials:

- Shoe boxes or other similar containers

Directions:

1. As a way of introducing the idea of souvenir or memory boxes to your students, have a class discussion about memories and how thoughts or objects can trigger them. Or, for younger students, read Mem Fox's book *Wilfrid Gordon McDonald Partridge* to your class.

2. Discuss how souvenirs remind us of other times and of places we have visited.

3. Explain to your students that they are invited to create souvenir boxes in which they will put objects that remind them of their learning. A souvenir might be a photograph, a recording of a poem or song, a rock from a science unit, a particularly challenging math problem the child solved, a favorite story, a video clip, and so forth.

Teacher Tips:

1. Allow students to keep journals or photo albums as souvenir holders.

2. Create a class souvenir box for a particular chapter/topic. Have each student contribute an object to the box. The student can either tag the object with a note explaining why it reminds him/her of the text, or explain the connection as part of a class discussion.

Exit Cards to Summarize

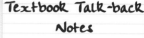

INDIVIDUAL   SMALL GROUP
PAIRS   WHOLE GROUP

Explanation:

This technique helps students reinforce what they have learned, as well as clarify their areas of interest in the topic. Exit cards also help teachers assess student progress and interest.

Materials:

- Index cards or student response journals

Directions:

1. Have students write either on index cards or in their journals.

2. Right before the end of class, give students five to ten minutes to write about the following:

    - Three things that I didn't know before and learned today are...

    - A question I still have is...

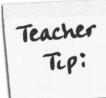

Teacher Tip:

1. Create a variety of exit cards that include different numbers and types of prompts for students to use. Students could write a poem, draw an illustration, or make an analogy before leaving that day's class. For example:

    a. In science, after studying volcanoes, you might ask your students to draw an illustration that captures at least three things they learned today.

    b. In history, you might have them write limericks about a military person they studied.

    c. In math, have them make up their own examples of problems studied that day and include the answers.

    d. Ask students to create riddles for others to answer about what was learned.

Textbook Talk-back Notes

Answer by the Number

Explanation:

This strategy will help struggling students focus on a smaller amount of text. This way they can more quickly locate information when answering end-of-the-chapter questions and not feel overwhelmed.

Materials:

- Post-it notes or nonpermanent tape

Directions:

1. Review the end-of-the-chapter questions and locate the paragraphs in the text that contain the answers.

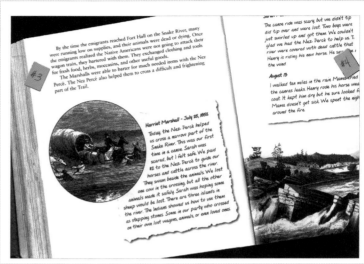

© 2002 National Geographic Society

2. Write each question number on a Post-it note or nonpermanent tape and place it in the margin beside the paragraph that contains the appropriate information with which to answer the question.

3. Cross-reference by placing an appropriate textbook page number by each question at the end of the chapter.

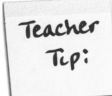

Teacher Tip:

1. Some higher-level, critical-thinking questions may not have a quick, "it's-in-this-one-paragraph" answer. For these you'll need to indicate when you cross-reference that there is more than one paragraph and/or page to look at when the students are searching for the information. This will then act as a signal to them that they need to combine information to answer the question.

Pieces of Eight

Textbook Talk-back Notes

Explanation:

This is a collaborative activity that allows students to review a concept or skill by moving around the room to collect other student responses, and writing them down on a sheet of paper folded into eight equal sections. In math, if the class is studying fact families of the number seven, a student's goal might be to get eight different equations that equal seven. In science, a student might gather eight different definitions for the unit's vocabulary words.

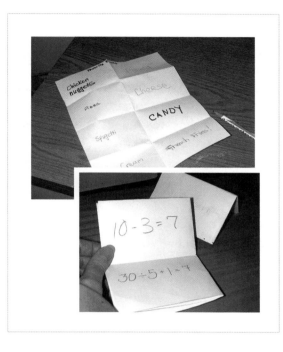

Materials:

- Paper
- Pencils

Directions:

1. For young students, model how to fold a sheet of paper into eight equal sections.

2. Have your students go to eight of their classmates and find out something about them—for example, each one's favorite food. Then they write the student's name and favorite food in one of the eight blank sections of their papers.

3. When all eight sections are filled in, have the students return to their seats and study their results individually or analyze them in a large group for patterns (e.g., for graphing the class's favorite foods).

4. Once you have practiced this activity with a simple task, use it in your content-area instruction for vocabulary definitions, skills reinforcement, main ideas, etc.

Teacher Tips:

1. Not all students will be able to fill in all eight sections, so you might want to do this the first few times with the paper folded into fourths, then increased to sixths, and finally eighths.

2. Have students create eight questions on the content they have read, write a question in each space on their sheet of paper, then move around the room and ask other students for their answers.

3. As students go around the room and ask their classmates questions, they, in turn, have to answer the questions that their classmates ask.

Four Corners Voting

Explanation:

This activity allows students to "vote with their feet" by choosing to stand in one of four corners or areas in the classroom, based on their commitment to their opinion about a question that was asked or a statement that was made. It keeps students moving around and thinking about what they are studying.

Directions:

1. Designate four corners or areas of the classroom where students can go to "vote with their feet." One will represent the opinion "Strongly Agree," the second will represent "Agree," the third "Disagree," and the fourth "Strongly Disagree."

2. Establish rules for student movement and behavior, such as: they should walk—not run—when they move from place to place; they should be respectful of their fellow classmates as they express their opinions; etc.

3. Practice this with your students first. You might say, "Show me how you feel about this statement: 'The school week should be extended to include Saturday mornings.' "

4. After students have moved to the corners of their choice to express initial opinions, request volunteers to defend their responses. When students listen to valid arguments or new information, give them the option to change their votes and walk to new corners.

5. Offer new information and/or scenarios to help students consider other perspectives.

Teacher Tip:

1. This activity requires a safe classroom environment, where students are comfortable taking overt risks and expressing how they feel.

Match-the-Meaning Card Game

INDIVIDUAL **SMALL GROUP**
PAIRS WHOLE GROUP

Explanation:

This activity is a fun way to keep kids motivated while they review textbook terminology and/or people.

Materials:

- Match-the-Meaning Cards reproducibles (see page 139)

Directions:

1. Make as many copies of the blank cards as you will need, keeping in mind that each term, date, or person's name will need two cards. (Use heavy stock or glue the cards to tagboard so words don't show through the paper.)

2. Write words or names on half of the blank cards.

3. Distribute sheets to pairs or small groups and ask them to provide appropriate definitions on the corresponding blank cards.

4. Once you've checked the answers for accuracy, laminate the sheets and cut them up into individual cards.

5. To play the game students shuffle the cards and deal the whole deck out to the players.

6. The goal of the game is to match the words with their definitions. As soon as the cards are dealt, students can look for matches in their hands and put those cards face up on the table. As play continues, each student draws a single card from the hand of the person to his/her left, then looks to see if this is a match for one he/she already has.

7. Players can challenge by using the textbook or the dictionary as a resource if they think someone has put down a bad match. If the match is wrong the player who put it down is out of the game and his/her cards are redistributed to the other players.

8. The game winner is the player who is out of cards first.

Teacher Tips:

1. For future reference you may want to indicate the textbook chapter or section number on the cards before you laminate them.

2. Save the cards to use for semester reviews.

Textbook Talk-back Notes

R.E.A.D.S. (RE-state, Answer, Details, State again)

Explanation:

This strategy provides students with a tool to help them write better responses to short-answer questions.

Directions:

1. Begin to teach the R.E.A.D.S. strategy by telling students that the first step in writing a good response to a short-answer question is to "re-state" the question. This is what the "R.E." refers to in the "R.E.A.D.S." acronym. Model this orally first, using a personal example. Follow with modeling a written restatement. For example, a question might be: "Why was the bald eagle selected as our national bird?" Restate: "There are several reasons why the bald eagle was selected as our national bird."

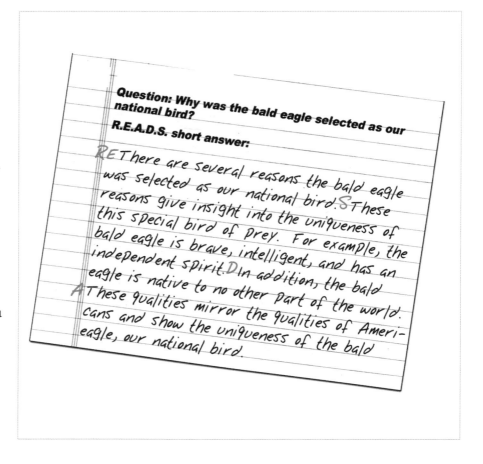

Question: Why was the bald eagle selected as our national bird?

R.E.A.D.S. short answer:

RE There are several reasons the bald eagle was selected as our national bird. **S** These reasons give insight into the uniqueness of this special bird of prey. For example, the bald eagle is brave, intelligent, and has an independent spirit. **D** In addition, the bald eagle is native to no other part of the world. **A** These qualities mirror the qualities of Americans and show the uniqueness of the bald eagle, our national bird.

2. Teach students the "A" or second step in the "R.E.A.D.S." acronym is for "answer." The student should now answer or respond to the restatement with a general statement. Students need to understand that a general statement means a main idea or topic sentence. Continue as in the first step above, modeling orally and in writing before asking students to attempt this on their own. For example, "The qualities of the bald eagle mirror the qualities of Americans and show the uniqueness of the bald eagle, our national bird." Point out to students that this statement needs to invite some details that will follow in the next step. The general answer or response in this step needs to make the reader want to say, "What do you mean?" or "Tell me more."

3. Explain to students that the "D" stands for "detail." Teach them that they now add one or two details, examples, or pieces of evidence to support the

"answer" statement in step two. For example, "The bald eagle is brave, intelligent, and has an independent spirit. In addition, the bald eagle is native to no other part of the world."

4. The last step in the "R.E.A.D.S." procedure is to write a statement (or statements) that "states again" or refers to the restatement of the question. For example, "These reasons give insight into the uniqueness of this special bird of prey."

Teacher Tip:

1. This strategy requires a lot of think-aloud modeling for students. Collect personal stories and low-level content materials such as familiar fairy tales, fables, or picture books to use to model each step of the process.

Textbook Look-back

Explanation:

Textbook Look-back helps students with fast-track searching and with finding specific information required to answer the end-of-the-chapter questions. Students should review these questions as a prerequisite to text skimming and looking back.

Materials:

- Textbook Look-back reproducible (see page 140)
- Overhead transparencies of textbook elements

Directions:

1. Create overhead transparencies of different elements in the textbook (e.g., headings, subheadings, topic sentences, captions, call-outs) and explain them to your students, discussing the importance and purpose of each.

2. Once your students have a clear understanding of these elements, have them skim over the text, keeping the chapter questions in mind, and:

   a. Try to recall when specific information was covered. Was it in the beginning, middle, or end of the chapter?

   b. Read the headings and subheadings to locate the right textbook page(s).

   c. Read the topic sentences to identify the specific paragraph where the information might be found.

   d. Read the captions under pictures, illustrations, charts, graphs, tables, diagrams, maps, and timelines.

   e. Read important vocabulary words in italics, set in boldface, and/or highlighted in a different color.

   f. Read any call-outs and sidebars.

3. For individual bookmarks, reproduce the form (see page 140) and laminate it. Make multiple copies available for students to self-monitor this strategy. Students can write on the laminated bookmarks with a dry-erase or water-soluble marker.

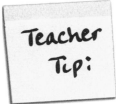

Teacher Tip:

1. Have a local copy service enlarge and laminate this Textbook Look-back form, which makes a great helping poster.

> **Textbook Lookback**
>
> I have skimmed over the text and . . .
>
> - read the heading and subheadings
> - read the topic sentences
> - read the captions of:
>   pictures
>   charts
>   diagrams
>   maps
>   illustrations
>   graphs
>   timelines
>   tables
> - identified and read important vocabulary terms
> - read the sidebars
> - read the call-outs

Writing Summaries

Textbook Talk-back
Notes

Explanation:

This strategy incorporates novelty and challenge into summary writing as students improve in their learning from textbook material. Eventually each student should be able to write a summary of an entire passage and develop independence in using this strategy.

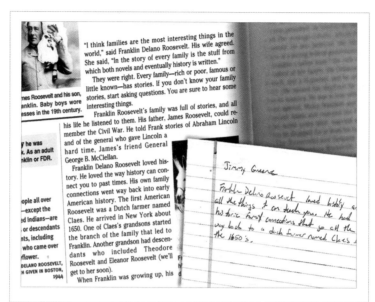

Directions:

1. Choose a short, appropriate passage from the textbook chapter students have read.

2. Group students into pairs and give each pair a copy of the first paragraph only from the selected passage, followed by 20 blank spaces.

3. Challenge each pair to write a summary of the paragraph in 20 words or less. Repeat this process with each paragraph.

4. Finally, ask students to combine two or three random 20-word summaries into one summary of 20 words or less.

Teacher Tip:

1. Make sure to select a passage consisting of a number of paragraphs, each containing enough information so that there is a main idea or gist to each one.

From A HISTORY OF US: WAR, PEACE, AND ALL THAT JAZZ (VOL 9) by Joy Hakim, © 1995 by Joy Hakim. Used by permission of Oxford University Press, Inc.

And That's the Rest of the Story

INDIVIDUAL
PAIRS

SMALL GROUP
WHOLE GROUP

Explanation:

Often textbook content is shallow and only teases the reader's interest in a topic, leaving too many questions unanswered. You can help expand content knowledge and bring the material more to life by providing students with extension activities and supplemental materials that complement the text topic.

Directions:

1. Encourage students to look beyond the information provided in the textbook and pursue some of the following activities:

    a. Go on field trips.
    b. Do Internet searches.
    c. Watch videos and movies.
    d. Conduct interviews.
    e. Bring in speakers.
    f. Read magazine articles, historical fiction, etc.
    g. Use encyclopedias or other reference books.

2. Do a read-aloud of interesting stories, curiosities, biographies, related articles, etc., that tie in with the topic.

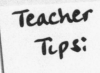

Teacher Tips:

1. This is an excellent opportunity for allowing students to work individually or in small, interest-based groups.

2. When possible, have students read or view material from primary sources, e.g., diaries, journals, letters, maps, photographs, etc. (see page 141).

3. Encourage students to brush up on background material before interviewing a person about his/her personal experience, e.g., Vietnam War, being a sea captain, fire fighting, etc.

4. Have students download material from several sources on the same topic and then compare and contrast the ideas and look for discrepancies.

Appendix
(Reproducibles)

Math Equivalents Cards

7/50	1/2	17/25	18/25
14%	50%	68%	72%
.14	.50	.68	.72

Math Equivalents Cards

9/20	81/100	1/4	1/5
45%	81%	25%	20%
.45	.81	.25	.20

Attribute Cards

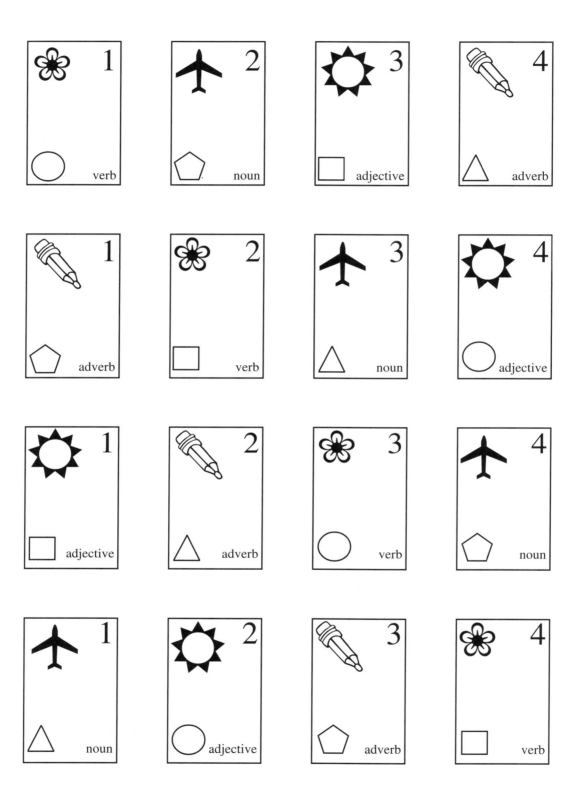

Pair Cards — States

New Hampshire	Texas	New Mexico
California	Delaware	Idaho
Maryland	Alaska	Alabama
Florida	New Jersey	Oregon
Kentucky	Michigan	West Virginia
Nevada	Massachusetts	Ohio

Pair Cards — States

Arkansas	Arizona	Colorado
Connecticut	Wyoming	Georgia
Hawaii	Kansas	Illinois
Indiana	Iowa	Louisiana
Maine	Minnesota	Mississippi
Missouri	Montana	Nebraska

Pair Cards — States

New York	North Carolina	North Dakota
Oklahoma	Pennsylvania	Rhode Island
South Carolina	South Dakota	Tennessee
Utah	Vermont	Virginia
Washington	Wisconsin	

Pair Cards — Capitals

Little Rock	Phoenix	Denver
Hartford	Cheyenne	Atlanta
Honolulu	Topeka	Springfield
Indianapolis	Des Moines	Baton Rouge
Augusta	Saint Paul	Jackson
Jefferson City	Helena	Lincoln

Pair Cards — Capitals

Concord	Austin	Santa Fe
Sacramento	Dover	Boise
Annapolis	Juneau	Montgomery
Tallahassee	Trenton	Salem
Frankfort	Lansing	Charleston
Carson City	Boston	Columbus

Pair Cards — Capitals

Albany	Raleigh	Bismarck
Oklahoma City	Harrisburg	Providence
Columbia	Pierre	Nashville
Salt Lake City	Montpelier	Richmond
Olympia	Madison	

Clock Partners

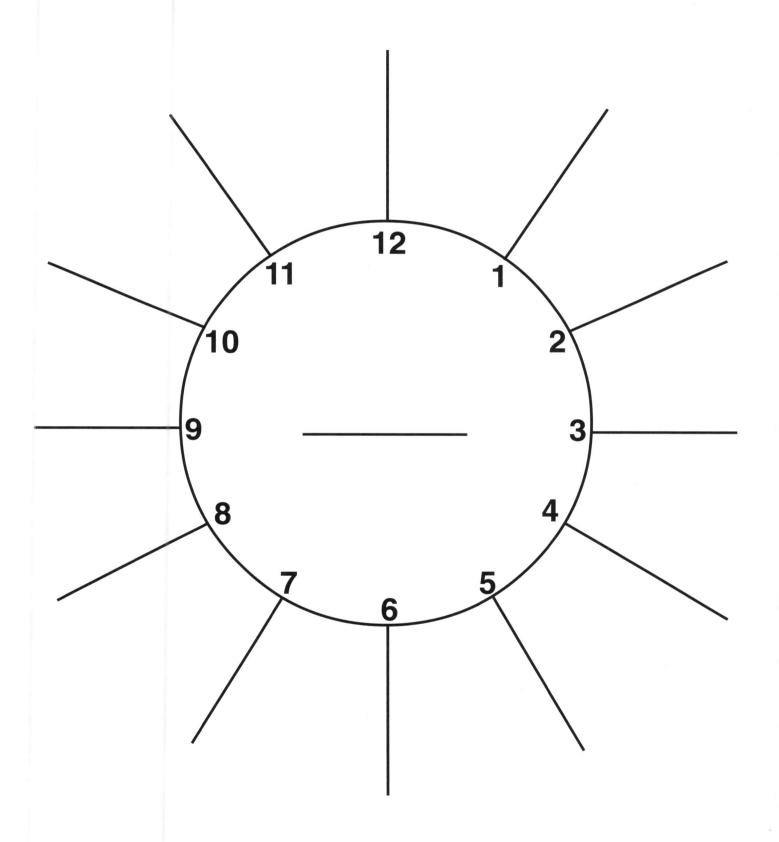

Circle of Three

I am 30. Where is 4 x 6?	**I am 24.** Where is 5 x 2?	**I am 10.** Where is 6 x 5?
I am 12. Where is 6 x 3?	**I am 18.** Where is 5 x 8?	**I am 40.** Where is 2 x 6?
I am 36. Where is 6 x 8?	**I am 48.** Where is 5 x 5?	**I am 25.** Where is 6 x 6?
I am 42. Where is 9 x 6?	**I am 54.** Where is 7 x 5?	**I am 35.** Where is 6 x 7?
I am 6. Where is 10 x 6?	**I am 60.** Where is 4 x 5?	**I am 20.** Where is 6 x 1?

Date: _____

Request Form for Permission to Copy or Record

Name: _____ **Title:** _____

School/Organization: _____

Address: _____

City: _____ **State:** _____ **Zip:** _____

Phone number: _____ **Fax number:** _____

E-mail address: _____

I would like to copy/record the following:

Title of Textbook: _____

Author(s): _____

Publisher: _____

Page number(s) for material to be reproduced: _____

Number of copies to be made: _____

My purpose for copying or recording this material is_____

_____

_____

_____

_____

_____

☐ The purpose is nonprofit   ☐ The purpose is for profit

Signature _____   Date _____

Textbook Adaptation Plan

Student _____ Date _____

Textbook Modifications

Goal: _____ _____ Modification: _____ _____ _____ _____ _____ _____ Implemented by: _____ Title/Role: _____	Progress Review Date: _____ Comments: _____ _____ _____ _____ _____ _____ _____ _____ _____
Goal: _____ _____ Modification: _____ _____ _____ _____ _____ _____ Implemented by: _____ Title/Role: _____	**Progress Review** Date: _____ Comments: _____ _____ _____ _____ _____ _____ _____ _____ _____
Goal: _____ _____ Modification: _____ _____ _____ _____ _____ _____ Implemented by: _____ Title/Role: _____	**Progress Review** Date: _____ Comments: _____ _____ _____ _____ _____ _____ _____ _____ _____

Textbook Adaptation Plan

Student _____   Date _____

Instructional Accommodations

Goal: _____
_____
Accommodation: _____
_____
_____
_____
_____

Implemented by: _____
Title/Role: _____

Progress Review

Date: _____

Comments: _____
_____
_____
_____
_____
_____
_____

Goal: _____
_____
Accommodation: _____
_____
_____
_____
_____

Implemented by: _____
Title/Role: _____

Progress Review

Date: _____

Comments: _____
_____
_____
_____
_____
_____
_____

Goal: _____
_____
Accommodation: _____
_____
_____
_____
_____

Implemented by: _____
Title/Role: _____

Progress Review

Date: _____

Comments: _____
_____
_____
_____
_____
_____
_____

Textbook Adaptation Plan

Student _____ Date _____

Additional Intervention Programs and Services

Goal: _____ _____ Program/Service: _____ _____ _____ _____ _____ Implemented by: _____ Title/Role: _____	**Progress Review** Date: _____ Comments: _____ _____ _____ _____ _____ _____ _____ _____
Goal: _____ _____ Program/Service: _____ _____ _____ _____ _____ _____ Implemented by: _____ Title/Role: _____	**Progress Review** Date: _____ Comments: _____ _____ _____ _____ _____ _____ _____ _____
Goal: _____ _____ Program/Service: _____ _____ _____ _____ _____ _____ Implemented by: _____ Title/Role: _____	**Progress Review** Date: _____ Comments: _____ _____ _____ _____ _____ _____ _____ _____

Concept Map

Topic: _____

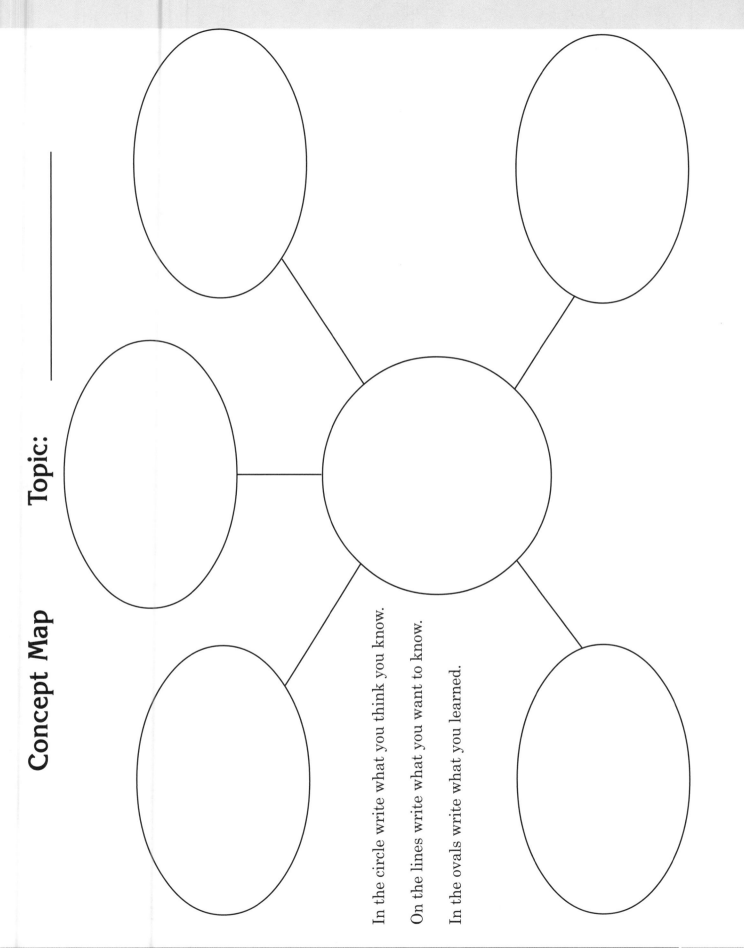

In the circle write what you think you know.

On the lines write what you want to know.

In the ovals write what you learned.

What I Know... What I Wonder... What I Learned

_____

Name   Date

_____

Topic or Unit of Study

What I know about	What I wonder about	What I learned about

Compacting Contract for _____

Extension topic:

_____

_____

Questions to be investigated:

_____

_____

_____

_____

Description of product of learning:

_____

_____

_____

Rules I will follow:

_____

_____

_____

Rubric or self-assessment tool and criteria:

4 _____

3 _____

2 _____

1 _____

_____   _____
Signature of Student   Date   Signature of Teacher   Date

Extension Activity Menu

Name: _____ Date: _____

I will show what I know by:	Plan Complete	Project Complete
writing a report		
making a booklet		
building a model		
doing a demonstration		
presenting a slide show		
videotaping a lesson		
telling a story		
writing a play		
making a map or chart		
painting a mural		
writing music		
writing and reciting a poem		
making a game		
mentoring a student		
Other: _____		

Compacting Record for _____

Academic Area	Unit of Study, Concept, or Skill	Documentation of Mastery	Extension Activity	Comments

Based on Joseph Renzulli's Curriculum Compacting, Creative Learning Press, 1993.

Pros, Cons, and What I Wonder

Name _____

Date _____

Topic _____

Pros	Cons	What I Wonder

Prefixes and Suffixes

PREFIXES

anti: (against) antisocial

audio: (to hear) audiocassette

auto: (self) autobiography

bi: (two) bi-level

de: (from) depart

dis: (not) disagree

en/em: (in, within) embed, enforce

flec/flex: (to bend) flexible

fract: (to break) fracture

in: (into, not) inactive

hydr: (water) hydroelectric

mis: (not) misspell

non: (not) nonfat

pre: (before) pretest

pro: (in favor of) prolong

re: (again) reappear

sub: (under, beneath) submarine

SUFFIXES

able: (inclined to) agreeable

ent: (one who) resident

er: (one who) speaker

est: (most) happiest

ful: (full of) boastful

gram: (writing, written) diagram

ion/tion: (state of) satisfaction

ject: (throw) reject

ly: (every) daily

less: (without) worthless

ment: (action or process) movement

meter: (instrument for measuring) thermometer

ness: (state of being) sadness

ology: (study of) geology

phone: (sound) telephone

scope: (instrument for viewing) telescope

SUFFIXES

able: (inclined to) agreeable

ent: (one who) resident

er: (one who) speaker

est: (most) happiest

ful: (full of) boastful

gram: (writing, written) diagram

ion/tion: (state of) satisfaction

ject: (throw) reject

ly: (every) daily

less: (without) worthless

ment: (action or process) movement

meter: (instrument for measuring) thermometer

ness: (state of being) sadness

ology: (study of) geology

phone: (sound) telephone

scope: (instrument for viewing) telescope

PREFIXES

anti: (against) antisocial

audio: (to hear) audiocassette

auto: (self) autobiography

bi: (two) bi-level

de: (from) depart

dis: (not) disagree

en/em: (in, within) embed, enforce

flec/flex: (to bend) flexible

fract: (to break) fracture

in: (into, not) inactive

hydr: (water) hydroelectric

mis: (not) misspell

non: (not) nonfat

pre: (before) pretest

pro: (in favor of) prolong

re: (again) reappear

sub: (under, beneath) submarine

SUFFIXES

able: (inclined to) agreeable

ent: (one who) resident

er: (one who) speaker

est: (most) happiest

ful: (full of) boastful

gram: (writing, written) diagram

ion/tion: (state of) satisfaction

ject: (throw) reject

ly: (every) daily

less: (without) worthless

ment: (action or process) movement

meter: (instrument for measuring) thermometer

ness: (state of being) sadness

ology: (study of) geology

phone: (sound) telephone

scope: (instrument for viewing) telescope

PREFIXES

anti: (against) antisocial

audio: (to hear) audiocassette

auto: (self) autobiography

bi: (two) bi-level

de: (from) depart

dis: (not) disagree

en/em: (in, within) embed, enforce

flec/flex: (to bend) flexible

fract: (to break) fracture

in: (into, not) inactive

hydr: (water) hydroelectric

mis: (not) misspell

non: (not) nonfat

pre: (before) pretest

pro: (in favor of) prolong

re: (again) reappear

sub: (under, beneath) submarine

Math Answer Estimates

Problem Number	Estimate	Actual Answer

Math Answer Estimates

Problem Number	Estimate	Actual Answer	Difference Between Estimate and Answer

Pointer/Signal Words

Sequence Text Structure: first, next, then, finally

Descriptive Text Structure: for example, to illustrate, such as, for instance

Problem and Solution Text Structure: dilemma, problem, puzzle, solved, the question is

Compare and Contrast Text Structure: alike, different, same as, different from, versus

Cause and Effect Text Structure: if . . . then, as a result, therefore, because

Pointer/Signal Words

Sequence Text Structure: first, next, then, finally

Descriptive Text Structure: for example, to illustrate, such as, for instance

Problem and Solution Text Structure: dilemma, problem, puzzle, solved, the question is

Compare and Contrast Text Structure: alike, different, same as, different from, versus

Cause and Effect Text Structure: if . . . then, as a result, therefore, because

Pointer/Signal Words

Sequence Text Structure: first, next, then, finally

Descriptive Text Structure: for example, to illustrate, such as, for instance

Problem and Solution Text Structure: dilemma, problem, puzzle, solved, the question is

Compare and Contrast Text Structure: alike, different, same as, different from, versus

Cause and Effect Text Structure: if . . . then, as a result, therefore, because

Keep-Your-Place Reading Tool Pattern

2" ½"

7"

Colored acetate attached to back of tagboard

1"

Colored acetate

2" ½"

7"

Colored acetate attached to back of tagboard

1"

Colored acetate

Self-Test for
Irlen Syndrome/Scotopic Sensitivity

Do you or someone you know have difficulty reading?
Take the following test:

	YES	NO
Do you skip words or lines when reading?		
Do you reread lines?		
Do you lose your place?		
Are you easily distracted when reading?		
Do you need to take breaks often?		
Do you find it harder to read the longer you read?		
Do you get headaches when you read?		
Do your eyes get red and watery?		
Does reading make you tired?		
Do you blink or squint?		
Do you prefer to read in dim light?		
Do you read close to the page?		
Do you use your finger or other markers?		
Do you get restless, active, or fidgety when reading?		

*If you answered *yes* to three or more of these questions, then you might be experiencing the effects of a perception problem called Irlen Syndrome/Scotopic Sensitivity and can be helped by the use of color (see www.Irlen.com).

Adapted with permission from Reading by the Colors *by Helen L. Irlen, Penguin Putnam/Perigee Div. Publishers.*

Focus Frame

DIRECTIONS:

Cut out and trace Focus Frame pattern below onto poster board or equivalent stock paper. Cut out focus frame from poster board, then cut along lines (indicated on pattern) on frame section A. Insert frame section B into section A to form a movable box. Slide the Focus Frame to adjust for the amount of space needed.

Student slides Focus Frame to fit the present problem.

Eliminates unnecessary information or distractions. →

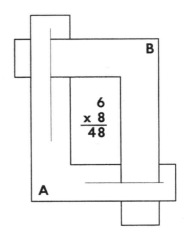

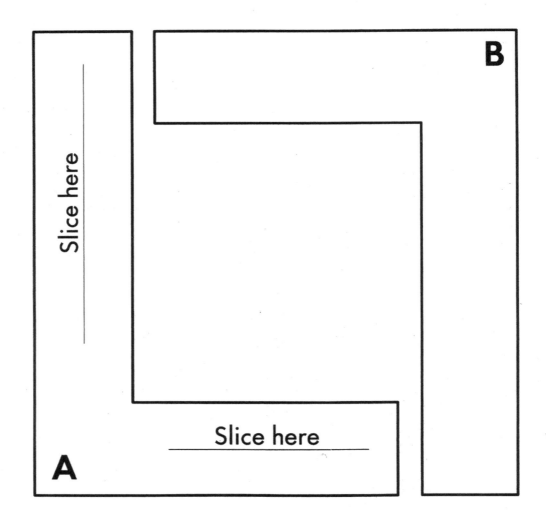

Active Bookmarks

Directions to Students:

On this sheet of paper are three bookmarks. Cut the bookmarks apart, then place one book-mark toward the front of the chapter, one bookmark toward the middle of the chapter, and one bookmark toward the end of the chapter. After you have placed your bookmarks, record the pages on this sheet in case the bookmarks fall out of the book. Please write the dates the book-marks are due. Enjoy your reading!

Your name: _____ Date: _____

Bookmark #1 page: _____ Due Date: _____

Bookmark #2 page: _____ Due Date: _____

Bookmark #3 page: _____ Due Date: _____

- -

Due Date: _____

Bookmark #1: Write about how the elements of the textbook (chapter headings, charts, foot-notes, etc.) have helped you understand what you are reading.

Name: _____ Page #: _____

- -

Due Date: _____

Bookmark #2: Make a graphic aid to help you understand what you have read to this point.

Name: _____ Page #: _____

- -

Due Date: _____

Bookmark #3: Describe what part of the information sticks in your mind.

Name: _____ Page #: _____

Content Puzzle

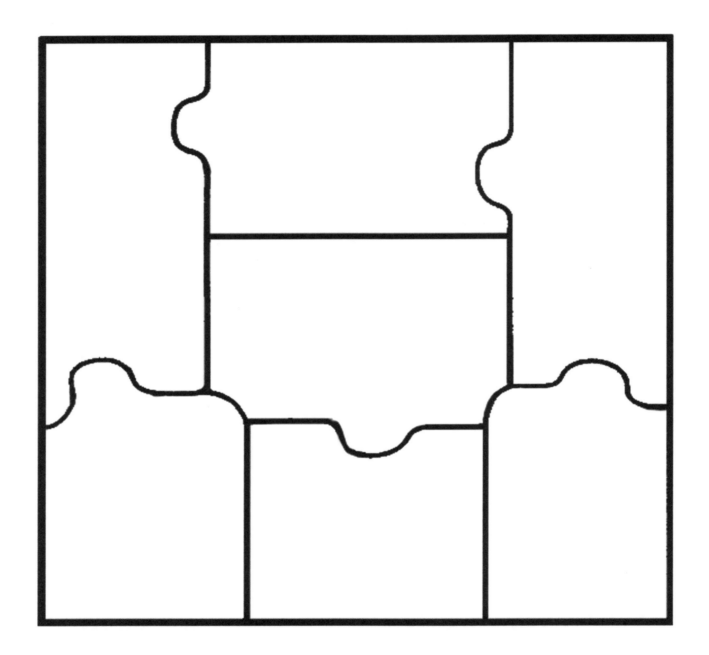

Compare/Contrast Text Structure

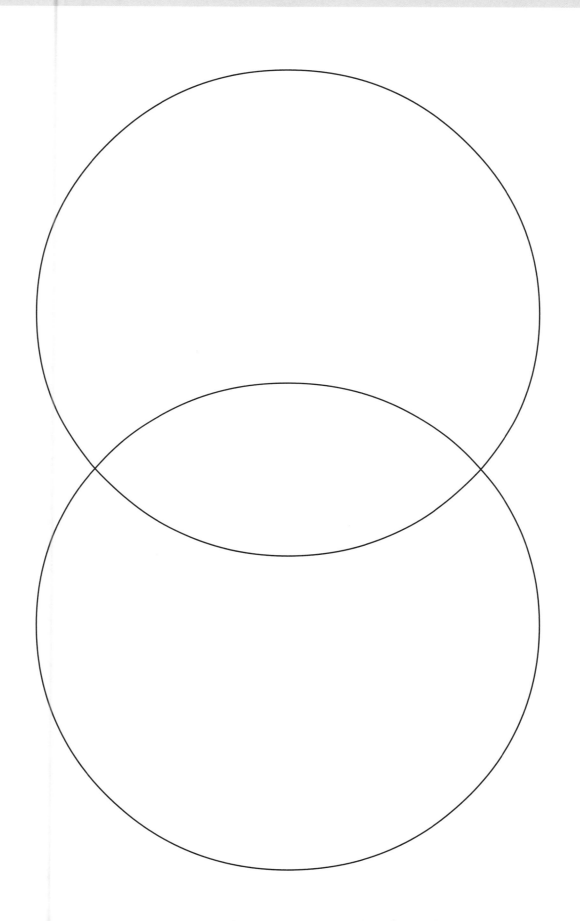

Descriptive Text Structure

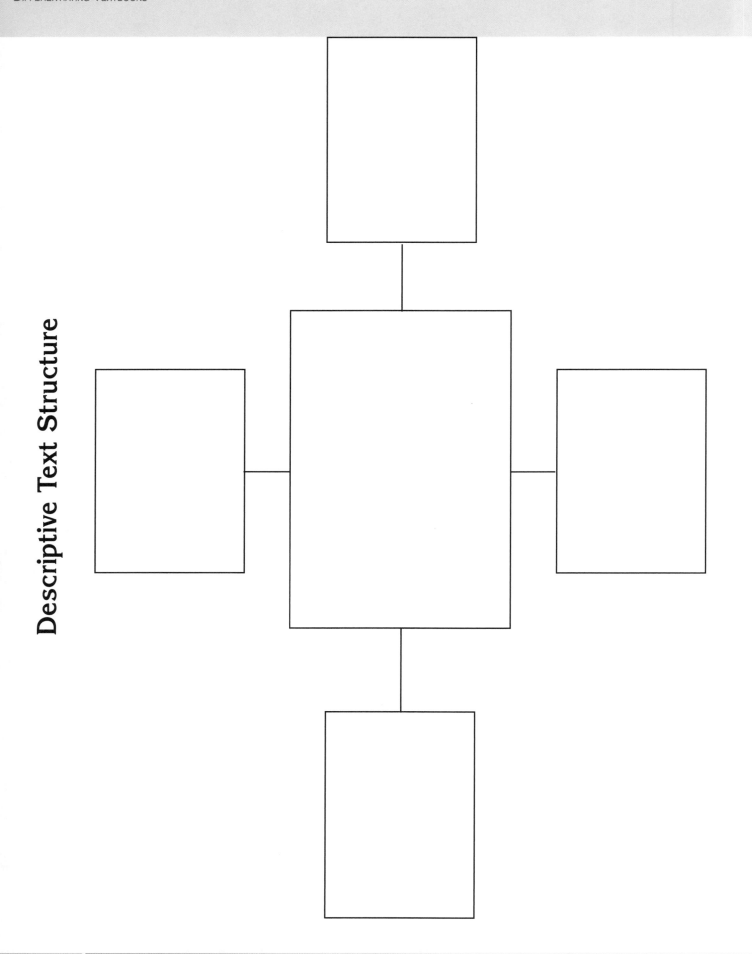

Cause/Effect Text Structure

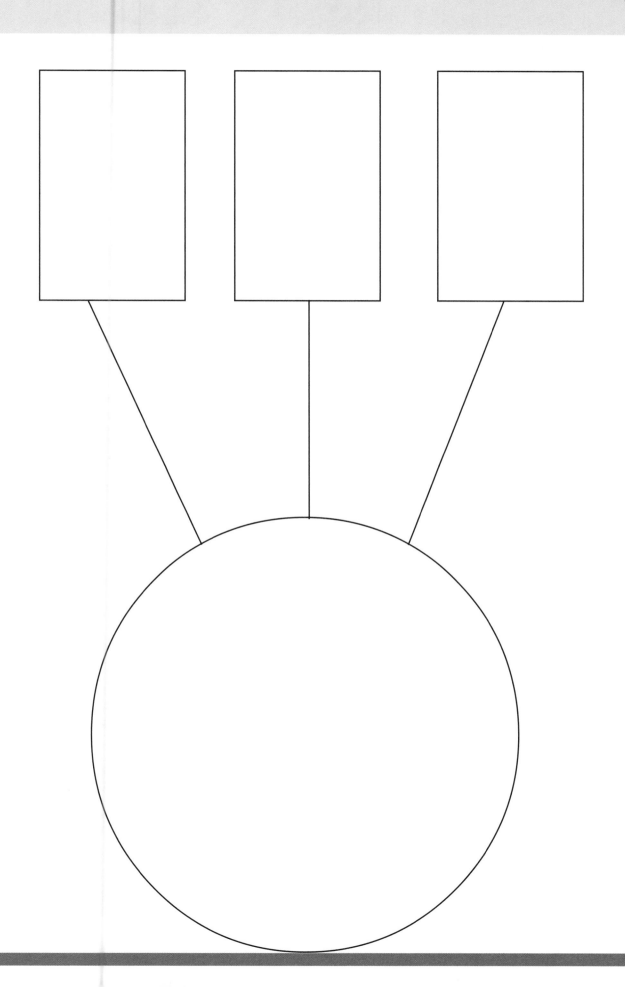

Problem/Solution Text Structure

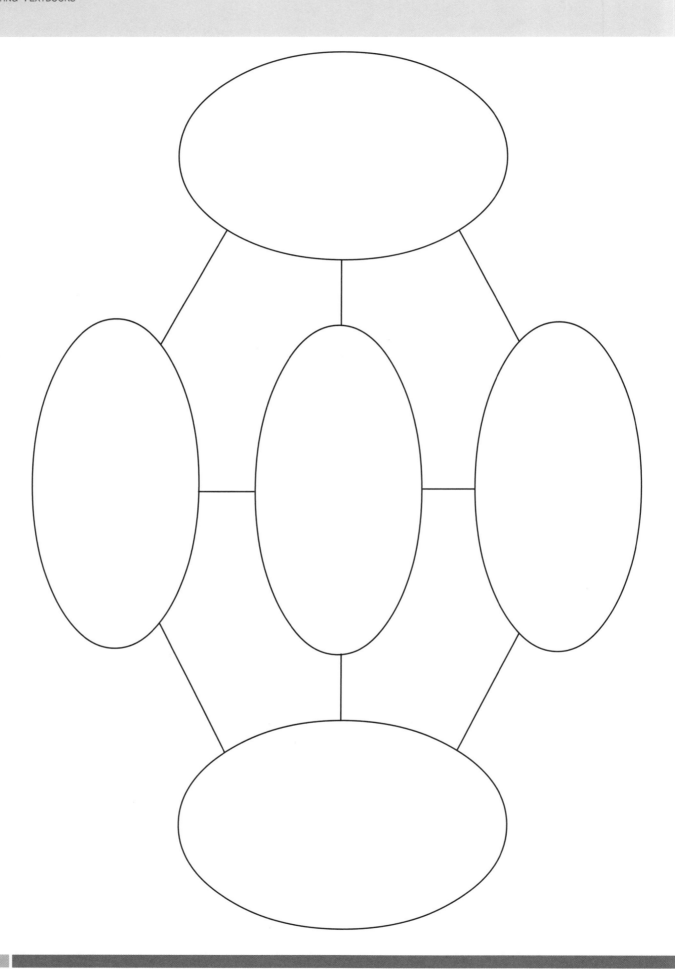

Sequence Text Structure

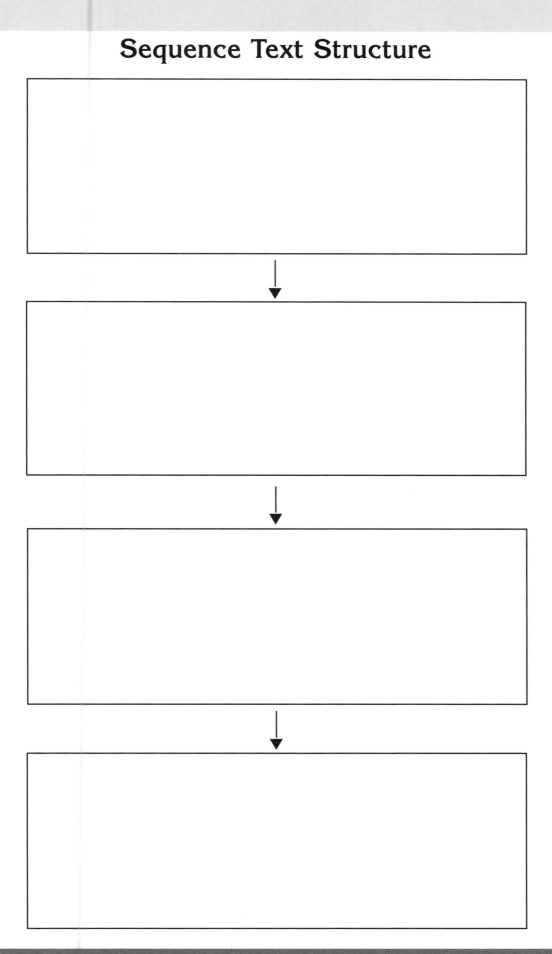

Textbook Talk-back Notes

Chapter _____ Page _____

Textbook Talk-back Notes

Chapter _____ Page _____

Textbook Talk-back Notes

Chapter _____ Page _____

Textbook Talk-back Notes

Chapter _____ Page _____

Math Word Problem Graphic Organizer

Name —————————————————————— Page # ——————————— Problem # ———————

Rewrite the problem in your own words.

Identify facts needed to solve the problem.

Write an equation and solve the problem.

Check your answer to see if it is reasonable.

Organizing, Categorizing, and Analyzing Grid

Category: _____

Features

Members

Symbols:

+ = yes   — = no   ? = don't know

Organizing, Categorizing, and Analyzing Grid

Category: _____

Features

Members

Symbols:

+ = yes   — = no   ? = don't know

Match-the-Meaning Cards

Textbook Look-back

I have skimmed over the text and . . .

- read the headings and subheadings

- read the topic sentences

- read the captions of:

  pictures

  charts

  diagrams

  maps

  illustrations

  graphs

  timelines

  tables

- identified and read important vocabulary terms

- read the sidebars

- read the call-outs

Textbook Look-back

I have skimmed over the text and . . .

- read the headings and subheadings

- read the topic sentences

- read the captions of:

  pictures

  charts

  diagrams

  maps

  illustrations

  graphs

  timelines

  tables

- identified and read important vocabulary terms

- read the sidebars

- read the call-outs

Textbook Look-back

I have skimmed over the text and . . .

- read the headings and subheadings

- read the topic sentences

- read the captions of:

  pictures

  charts

  diagrams

  maps

  illustrations

  graphs

  timelines

  tables

- identified and read important vocabulary terms

- read the sidebars

- read the call-outs

Textbook Look-back

I have skimmed over the text and . . .

- read the headings and subheadings

- read the topic sentences

- read the captions of:

  pictures

  charts

  diagrams

  maps

  illustrations

  graphs

  timelines

  tables

- identified and read important vocabulary terms

- read the sidebars

- read the call-outs

Finding the Evidence Through Primary Sources*

Letters
Diaries
Maps
Period clothing
Early toys
Newspaper clippings
Old posters
Photographs
Newsreels
Blueprints
Illustrations
Old postcards
Documents
Relics, artifacts, antiques, etc.
Old tools
Eyewitness accounts
Drawings
Audio recordings
Videos

*Material created at the time history was being made.

Resources

REFERENCE WORKS AND RESEARCH

Allen, Janet. *It's Never Too Late*. Portsmouth, NH: Heinemann, 1995.

————. *On the Same Page*. Portland, ME: Stenhouse Publishers, 2002.

————. *Words, Words, Words*. Portland, ME: Stenhouse Publishers, 1999.

————. *Yellow Brick Roads: Shared and Guided Paths to Independent Reading 4-12*. Portland, ME: Stenhouse Publishers, 2000.

Allen, Janet and Kyle Gonzalez. *There's Room for Me Here*. Portland, ME: Stenhouse Publishers, 1998.

Allington, Richard L. *What Really Matters for Struggling Readers: Designing Research-Based Programs*. New York: Longman, 2001.

Alllington, Richard L. and Patricia M. Cunningham. *Schools That Work: Where All Children Read and Write*. New York: HarperCollins Publishers, 1996.

Anderson, T.H. and B.B. Armbruster. Content area textbooks. In *Learning to Read in American Schools*, edited by R.C. Anderson, J. Osborne, and R.J. Tierney. Hillsdale, NJ: Erlbaum, 1984.

Armbruster, B.B. "Mapping: An Innovative Reading and Comprehension Study Strategy." Paper presented at the Annual Meeting of the American Educational Research Association, Boston, MA, 1980.

Armbruster, B.B. and T.H. Anderson. On selecting "considerate content area textbooks." *Remedial and Special Education,* 9, no. 1 (1988): 47-52.

Armbruster, B.B. and B. Gudbrandsen. "Reading Comprehension in Social Studies Programs." *Reading Research Quarterly,* 21 (1986): 36-48.

Armbruster, B.B., J.H. Osborne, and A.L. Davison. "Readability Formulas May Be Dangerous to Your Textbooks." *Educational Leadership,* 42 (1985): 18-20.

Aronson, Elliot and S. Patnoe. *The Jigsaw Classroom*. New York: Addison-Wesley Longman, 1997.

Barton, Mary Lee and Claire Heidema. *Teaching Reading in Mathematics*. Aurora, CO: McREL, 2000.

Bender, William N. *Differentiating Instruction for Students with Learning Disabilities*. Thousand Oaks, CA: Corwin Press, Inc., 2002.

Benjamin, Amy. *Differentiated Instruction: A Guide for Middle and High School Teachers*. Larchmont, NY: Eye on Education, 2002.

Bennett, Barrie and Carol Rolheiser. *Beyond Monet: The Artful Science of Instructional Integration*. Toronto: Bookation Inc., 2001.

Billmeyer, Rachel and Mary Lee Barton. *Teaching in the Content Areas: If Not Me, Then Who?* Aurora, CO: McREL, 1998.

Bromley, Karen, Linda Irwin DeVitis, and Marcial Modlo. *50 Graphic Organizers for Reading, Writing & More*. New York: Scholastic Inc., 1999.

Buehl, Doug. *Classroom Strategies for Interactive Learning*. Newark, DE: International Reading Association, 2001.

Buzan, Tony. *The Mind Map Book.* Woodlands, London: BBC Books, 1993.

Campbell, Bruce. *The Multiple Intelligences Handbook.* Stanwood, WA: Campbell & Assoc., Inc., 1994.

Ciborowski, Jean. *Textbooks and the Students Who Can't Read Them.* Cambridge, MA: Brookline Books, 1992.

Cole, Ardith Davis. *Better Answers: Written Performance That Looks Good and Sounds Smart.* Portland, ME: Stenhouse, 2002.

Culham, Ruth. *6 + 1 Traits of Writing.* New York: Scholastic Inc., 2002.

Cummings, Carol. *Winning Strategies for Classroom Management.* Arlington, VA: ASCD, 2000.

Curtis, Mary E. and Ann Marie Longo. *When Adolescents Can't Read: Methods and Materials That Work.* Cambridge, MA: Brookline Books, 1998.

Dakos, Kalli. *Don't Read This Book, Whatever You Do!* New York: Simon & Schuster, 1993.

Daniels, Harvey. *Literature Circles: Voice and Choice in the Student-Centered Classroom.* Portland, ME: Stenhouse, 1994.

Flynn, Kris. *Graphic Organizers…Helping Children Think Visually.* Cypress, CA: Creative Teaching Press, 1995.

Forsten, Char, Jim Grant, and Betty Hollas. *Differentiated Instruction: Different Strategies for Different Learners.* Peterborough, NH: Crystal Springs Books, 2002.

Fox, Mem. *Wilfrid Gordon McDonald Partridge.* Brooklyn, NY: Kane/Miller, 1985.

Fry, Edward. *How to Teach Reading.* Westminster, CA: Teacher Created Materials, 1995.

Gardner, Howard. *Frames of Mind.* New York: Basic Books, Inc., 1983.

Gibbs, Jeanne. *Tribes: A Process for Social Development and Cooperative Learning.* Santa Rosa, CA: Center Source Publications, 1987.

Grant, Jim. *Retention and It's Prevention.* Rosemont, NJ: Modern Learning Press, 1997.

———. *Struggling Learners: Below Grade or Wrong Grade?* Rosemont, NJ: Modern Learning Press. 2002.

Grant, Jim and Char Forsten. *If You're Riding a Horse and It Dies, Get Off.* Peterborough, NH: Crystal Springs Books, 1999.

Grant, Jim and Irv Richardson. *The Retention/Promotion Checklist.* Peterborough, NH: Crystal Springs Books, 1998.

Gregory, Gayle H. and Carolyn Chapman. *Differentiated Instructional Strategies.* Thousand Oaks, CA: Corwin Press, Inc., 2002.

Hakim, Joy. *A History of US.* (10-book series). New York: Oxford University Press., 1995.

Harvey, Stephanie. *Nonfiction Matters: Reading, Writing, and Research in Grades 3-8.* Portland, ME: Stenhouse Publishers, 1998.

Harvey, Stephanie, and A. Gouvis. *Strategies That Work: Teaching Comprehension to Enhance Understanding.* York, ME: Stenhouse Publishers, 2000.

Heacox, Diane. *Differentiating Instruction in the Regular Classroom.* Minneapolis, MN: Free Spirit Press, 2002.

Herber, H.L. *Teaching Reading in the Content Areas.* 2nd ed. Englewood Cliffs, NJ: Prentice-Hall, 1978.

Hoyt, Linda. *Make It Real: Strategies for Success with Informational Texts.* Portsmouth, NH: Heinemann, 2002.

Irlen, Helen. *Reading by the Colors.* Garden City Park, NY: Avery Publishing Group Inc., 1991.

Irvin, Judith. *Reading and the Middle School Students: Strategies to Enhance Literacy.* Boston: Allyn Bacon, 1998.

———. *Reading Strategies for the Social Studies Classroom.* Austin, TX: Holt, Rhinehart, and Winston.

Jensen, Eric. *Brain Compatible Strategies.* San Diego, CA: The Brain Store, Inc., 1998.

———. *Different Brains, Different Learners.* San Diego, CA: The Brain Store, Inc., 2000.

———. *Music with the Brain in Mind.* San Diego, CA: The Brain Store, Inc., 2000.

Johnson, D.W., and R.T. Johnson. *Learning Together and Alone: Cooperative, Competitive, Individualistic Learning.* Boston, MA: Allyn & Bacon, 1994.

Kagan, Miguel, Laurie Robertson, and Spencer Kagan. *Cooperative Learning Structures for Classroom Building.* San Clemente, CA: Kagan Publishing and Professional Development, 1995.

Kagan, Spencer. *Cooperative Learning.* San Clemente, CA: Kagan Publishing and Professional Development, 1994.

Keene, Ellin Oliver and Susan Zimmermann. *Mosaic of Thought.* Portsmouth, NH: Heinemann, 1997.

Kotulak, Ronald. *Inside the Brain.* Kansas City, MO: Andrews McMeel Publishing, 1996.

Levine, Mel. *A Mind at a Time.* New York: Simon & Schuster, 2002.

Marzano, Robert J., Jennifer S. Norford, Diane E. Paynter, Debra J. Pickering, and Barbara B. Gaddy. *Classroom Instruction That Works.* Arlington, VA: Association for Supervision and Curriculum Development, 2001.

McKenna, Michael C. *Help for Struggling Readers: Strategies for Grades 3-8.* New York, NY: The Guilford Press, 2002.

Miller, Debbie. *Reading with Meaning: Teaching Comprehension in the Primary Grades.* Portland, ME: Stenhouse Publishers, 2002.

Moore, David W., Donna E. Alvermann, and Kathleen A. Hinchmann, editors. *Struggling Adolescent Readers: A Collection of Teaching Strategies.* Newark, DE: International Reading Association, 2000.

The National Education Commission on Time and Learning (updated for 2000 by Staff Development for Educators). *Prisoners of Time.* Peterborough, NH: Crystal Springs Books, 2000.

Ogle, Donna. K-W-L: A teaching model that develops active reading of expository text. *The Reading Teacher,* 39 (1986): 564-570.

Ohanian, Susan. *What Happened to Recess and Why Are Our Children Struggling in Kindergarten?* New York: McGraw-Hill, 2002.

Paul, Korky and Valerie Thomas. *Winnie the Witch.* Brooklyn, NY: Kane/Miller Book Publishers, 1987.

Payne, Ruby. *A Framework for Understanding Poverty.* Baytown, TX: RFT Publishing Co., 1998.

Raphael, Taffy. "Question-Answer Strategy for Children." *The Reading Teacher*, 36 (1982): 303-311.

Readence, J., D. Moore, and R. Rickelman. *Prereading Activities for Content Area Reading and Learning.* 3rd ed. Newark, DE: International Reading Association, 2000.

"Reading at the Middle and High School Levels: Building Active Readers Across the Curriculum." 2nd ed. Arlington, VA: Education Research Service, 1999.

Reavis, George H. *The Animal School.* (Foreword and Epilogue by Char Forsten, Jim Grant, and Irv Richardson). Peterborough, NH: Crystal Springs Books, 1999.

Reis, Sally, Deborah Burns, and Joseph S. Renzulli. *Curriculum Compacting.* Mansfield Center, CT: Creative Learning Press, Inc., 1992.

Robb, Laura. *Teaching Reading in Middle School: A Strategic Approach to Teaching Reading That Improves Comprehension and Thinking.* New York: Scholastic Inc., 2000.

————. *Teaching Reading in Social Studies, Science, and Math: Practical Ways to Weave Comprehension Strategies Into Your Content Area Teaching.* New York, NY: Scholastic Inc., 2003.

Rumelhart, D. *Toward an Interactive Model of Reading.* (Tech. Rep. No. 56). San Diego, CA: University of California Center for Human Information Processing, 1976.

Rutherford, Paula. *Instruction for All Students.* Alexandria, VA: Just ASK Publications, 2002.

Santa, C. *Content Reading Including Study Systems.* Dubuque, Iowa: Kendall/Hunt, 1988.

Santa, C., L. Havens, and E. Macumber. *Creating Independence Through Student-Owned Strategies.* Dubuque, Iowa: Kendall/Hunt, 1996.

Saphier, Jon and R. Gower. *The Skillful Teacher: Building Your Teaching Skills.* Carlisle, MA: Research for Better Teaching, 1983.

Silver, Debbie. *Drumming to the Beat of a Different Marcher.* Nashville, TN: Incentive Publications, Inc., 2003.

Slavin, Robert. *Cooperative Learning.* Needham Heights, MA: Allyn & Bacon, 1995.

Smith, Michael W. and Jeffrey D. Wilhelm. *"Reading Don't Fix No Chevys."* Portsmouth, NH: Heinemann, 2002.

Smith, P. and G. Tompkins. *"Structured Notetaking: A New Strategy for Content Area Readers."* Journal of Reading, 32 (1988): 46-53.

Sousa, David. *How the Gifted Brain Learns.* Thousand Oaks, CA: Corwin Press, Inc., 2003.

————. *How the Special Needs Brain Learns.* Thousand Oaks, CA: Corwin Press, Inc., 2001.

Strickland, D., Kathy Ganske, and Joanne K. Monroe. *Supporting Struggling Readers and Writers: Strategies for Classroom Interventions 3-6.* Portland, ME: Stenhouse Publishers and Newark, DE: International Reading Association, 2002.

Swanson, Philip N. and Susan De La Paz. "Teaching Effective Comprehension Strategies to Students with Learning and Reading Disabilities." *Intervention in School and Clinic*, 33, no. 4 (1998): 209-218.

Thurlow, Martha L., Judy L. Elliott, and James E. Ysseldyke. *Testing Students with Disabilities, Practical Strategies for Complying with District and State Requirements.* Thousand Oaks, CA: Corwin Press, Inc., 2002.

Tomlinson, Carol Ann. *The Differentiated Classroom Responding to the Needs of All Learners.* Alexandria, VA: ASCD, 1999.

————. *How to Differentiate Instruction in Mixed Ability Classrooms.* Alexandria, VA: ASCD, 2001.

Tomlinson, Carol Ann and Susan Allan Demirsky. *Leadership for Differentiating Schools & Classrooms.* Alexandria, VA: ASCD, 2002.

Tomlinson, Carol Ann, Sandra N. Kaplan, Joseph S. Renzulli, Jeanne Purcell, Jann Leppien, and Deborah Burns. *The Parallel Curriculum.* Thousand Oaks, CA: Corwin Press, 2002.

Tovani, Chris and Ellin Oliver Keene. *I Read It, But I Don't Get It.* York, ME: Stenhouse Publisers, 2000.

Tyson-Bernstein, Harriet. *A Conspiracy of Good Intentions: America's Textbook Fiasco.* Washington, DC: The Council for Basic Education, 1988.

Winebrenner, Susan. *Teaching Gifted Kids in the Regular Classroom.* Minneapolis, MN: Free Spirit Press, 1992.

————. *Teaching Kids with Learning Difficulties in the Regular Classroom.* Minneapolis, MN: Free Spirit Publishing, Inc., 1996.

Witherell, Nancy L. and Mary C. McMackin. *Graphic Organizers and Activities for Differentiated Instruction in Reading.* New York: Scholastic Inc., 2002.

PRODUCTS, SUPPLIES, AND ADAPTIVE SERVICES

Aural and visual aids, and tools for learning difficulties are available from:

The American Printing House for the Blind
P.O. Box 6085
Louisville, KY 40206-0085
1-800-223-1839 (phone)
1-502-899-2274 (fax)
www.aph.org

Califone International, Inc.
21300 Superior Street
Chatsworth, CA 91311
800-722-0500 (phone)
818-407-2405 (fax)
www.califone.com
The CardMaster® plus other sound equipment and accessories.

HEARIT COMPANY
180 W. Magee Road, Suite 152
Tucson, AZ 85704
800-298-7184 (phone)
520-579-3368 (fax)
www.hearitllc.com
Tools that amplify the frequencies in the voice/ speech range to improve speech discrimination for individuals with undetected or slight hearing loss, language/learning disabilities, and ADD/ ADHD.

Kurzweil Education Systems
14 Crosby Drive
Bedford, MA 01730-1402
800-894-5374 (phone)
781-276-0650 (fax)
www.kurzweiledu.com
Reading and writing software for individuals with learning difficulties and for those who are blind.

Library Reproduction Services (LRS)
14214 South Figueroa Street
Los Angeles, CA 10061-1034
1-800-255-5002
www.lrs-largeprint.com
Large-print textbooks.

National Library Service for the Blind and Physically Handicapped
The Library of Congress
1291 Taylor Street N.W.
Washington, DC 20542
www.loc.gov/nls
Custom produced books (Braille, audio recording, and large print).

RFB&D
20 Roszel Road
Princeton, NJ 08340
800-221-4792 (phone)
609-987-8116 (fax)
www.rfbd.org
Recordings for the blind and dyslexic.

Colored overlays are available from:

Crystal Springs Books
75 Jaffrey Road, P.O. Box 500
Peterborough, NH 03458
1-800-321-0401
www.crystalsprings.com
and
The Irlen Institute
5380 Village Road
Long Beach, CA 90808
562-496-2550
www.irlen.com

Highlighting tape is available from many teacher-supply stores and from:

Crystal Springs Books
75 Jaffrey Road, P.O. Box 500
Peterborough, NH 03458
1-800-321-0401
www.crystalsprings.com

Recorded books, tape recorders, multiple headset jack boxes, and headphones are available from:

The National Reading Styles Institute
P.O. Box 737
Syosset, NY 11791
1-800-331-3117
and
Recorded Books, Inc.
270 Skipjack Road
Prince Frederick, MD 20678
800-638-1304
410-535-5499 (fax)
www.recordedbooks.com
Publisher of audio books for K-12 educators and
    librarians; and for personal use—rent or buy.

Study carrels are available from:

Quality Learning Enterprises
P.O. Box 385
Joshua Tree, CA 92252
760-366-3441 (phone)
760-366-1292 (fax)
www.qualitylearningenterprises.com
"The Concentration Station"

Ten-minute tapes are available from:

Crystal Springs Books
75 Jaffrey Road, P.O. Box 500
Peterborough, NH 03458
1-800-321-0401
www.crystalsprings.com

Professional development and curricular materials are available from:

Association for Supervision & Curriculum
    Development
1703 North Beauregard Street,
Alexandria, VA 22311-1714
1-800-933-ASCD (phone)
1-703-575-5400 (fax)
www.ascd.org

Crystal Springs Books
75 Jaffrey Road, P.O. Box 500
Peterborough, NH 03458
1-800-321-0401
www.crystalsprings.com
The "where-house" of teacher books and materials.

Interact
5937 Darwin Court, Suite 106
Carlsbad, CA 92008
800-359-0961 (telephone)
800-700-5093 (fax)
www.interact-simulations.com
Comprehensive thematic, hands-on units of study for
    all grade levels in all academic areas.

Lakeshore®
2695 E. Dominguez Street
Carson, CA 90810
800-421-5354 (phone)
310-537-5403 (fax)
www.lakeshorelearning.com

Learning materials and educational products ranging from language and literacy to science and mathematics; furniture and art materials to puzzles, hands-on learning kits, and products that focus on multiculturalism and special needs; for early childhood, elementary, high school, and adult education.

National Geographic
P.O. Box 98199
Washington, DC 20090-8199
1-800-647-5463 (phone)
www.nationalgeographic.com

Oxford University Press USA
198 Madison Avenue
New York, NY 10016
1-212-726-6000 (phone)
www.oup-usa.org

Staff Development for Educators (SDE)
10 Sharon Road, P.O. Box 577
Peterborough, NH 03458
1-800-924-9621 (phone)
www.sde.com

Teacher Created Materials
641 Industry Way
Westminster, CA 92683
714-891-2273 (phone)
714-892-0283 (fax)
www.teachercreated.com

Teacher's Curriculum Institute
P.O. Box 1327
Rancho Cordova, CA 95741
800-297-5138 (telephone)
www.teachtci.com

Products created by and for teachers to help them engage all learners in their diverse classrooms.

EDUCATIONAL ORGANIZATIONS

National Association for Elementary School Principals
1615 Duke Street
Alexandria, VA 22314
1-800-386-2377
www.naesp.org

National Association of Secondary School Principals
1904 Association Drive
Reston, VA 20191-1537
1-703-860-0200
www.nassp.org

National Council for the Social Studies
8555 Sixteenth Street, Suite 500
Silver Spring, MD 20910
301-588-1800 (phone)
301-588-2049 (fax)
www.ncss.org

National Council of Teachers of Mathematics
1906 Association Drive
Reston, VA 20191-1502
1-703-620-9840 (phone)
1-703-476-2970 (fax)
www.nctm.org

National Council of Teachers of English

1111 W. Kenyon Road

Urbana, IL 61801-1096

1-800-369-6283 (phone)

1-217-328-9645 (fax)

www.ncte.org

US Department of Education

400 Maryland Avenue SW

Washington, DC 20202

1-800-USA-LEARN (phone)

1-202-401-0689 (fax)

HELPFUL WEB SITES

Literacy and More

www.lauracandler.com

Numerous ideas to enrich your literacy classroom.

www.readingAtoZ.com—download

Pre-leveled books to use in your reading instructions, ranging from pre-primer to fifth-grade levels.

www.educatorsoutlet.com

Many manipulatives at discounted prices.

www.sopriswest.com

Highly effective supplemental materials and programs for struggling students.

www.TeachingIsEasy.com

Customize your own activities and games around your specific reading, math, and science vocabulary words. Good for ESL and bilingual teachers, too.

Math, Science, Social Studies

www.boxcarsandoneeyedjacks.com

Source of math and spelling games and materials.

www.cobblestonepub.com

Publisher of high-interest social studies and science magazines for all grade levels.

www.saxonpublishers.com/activities/basic_fact_sheets/index.html

Free webpage allows students to take timed math facts while online. Teachers or students can choose the type of operations, the number of problems, and the target time. The web site does the rest. It provides immediate feedback to students regarding accuracy and speed.

www.SciLinks.org ; www.nsta.org

In partnership with major publishers, the National Science Teachers Association has launched a program called SciLinks, which makes the Internet a more powerful and relevant learning tool and represents a cutting-edge method of assisting teachers, students, and parents in the science teaching and learning process.

www.singaporemath.com

View and purchase Singapore math textbooks from this site in Portland, Oregon.

Teacher/Training Tools

www.trainerswarehouse.com

www.creativetrainingtechniques.com

www.ustoy.com

These sites offer motivational teaching tools and gadgets that make presentations come alive!

www.kidcrosswords.com

www.puzzlemaker.school.discovery.com

Sites for crossword puzzles, but many more are available by doing a search through Google for "children's crossword puzzles."

www.thelefthand.com

www.io.com/~cortese/left/southpaw.html

Suppliers of rulers, notebooks, pencils, etc., specifically designed for left-handed persons.

Index

A

Adapting textbooks, strategies for: circle and box math problems, 28; eliminating unnecessary information, 27; laminated chapter books, 24; large-print textbooks, 29; photocopied chapter books, 25; rewriting headings and subheadings, 26; textbook adaptation plan, 30, 114-16

Addition problems, reducing errors in, 28

After-reading strategies, xii; for answering questions, 89, 92, 96-97, 98; for committing information to long-term memory, 85; for expanding content knowledge, 100, 141; for expressing opinions, 94; for finding literal vs. inferential answers, 82-83; for homework support, 79; for organizing, categorizing, and analyzing information, 81, 138; for processing information, 86, 88; purpose of, 77; for responding to textbook questions, 78; for reviewing concept or skill, 93; for reviewing text, 88, 90; for rewriting headings and subheadings, 26; for summarizing textbook information, 84, 91, 99; for vocabulary help, 80, 87, 95, 139

Anchor activities, 18, 22, 40, 41

Answers: to end-of-chapter questions, 92; homework, giving all or part of, 79; literal vs. inferential, 82-83; math, estimating, 51, 124

Anticipation Guide, for motivating students to read textbook, 43

Art, pairing students in, 18

Attribute cards: for creating groups of four, 16-17; reproducible for, 104

Audiocassettes: for recorded textbooks, 64; for taped responses, 89; for taped vocabulary words, 39

Auditory distractions, headphones reducing, 65

B

Before-reading strategies, xii; activating prior knowledge about material, 32-33, 53, 117; estimating math answers, 51, 124; highlighting text, 54; improving comprehension of textbook, 48; introducing vocabulary, 37-42, 123; motivating students to read textbook, 43, 53; predicting and setting purposes for reading, 45-47; pre-reading textbook chapter, 52, 125; purpose of, 31; setting purpose for reading, 36, 122; summarizing knowledge of subject, 44; teaching material not yet mastered, 34-35, 118-21; visual aids, 49-50

Bookmarks, active: for focusing on text, 61; reproducible for, 129

Boxing math problems, for reducing computation errors, 28

C

Card games: for grouping students, 21-22; for reviewing vocabulary, 95

Chapter books: laminated, as textbook adaptation, 24; photocopied, as textbook adaptation, 25

Charades, for vocabulary review, 87

Circle of Three: for grouping students, 20; reproducible for, 112

Circling math problems, for reducing computation errors, 28

Clock Partners: for pairing students, 19; reproducible for, 111

Cloze activity, for predicting and setting purposes for reading, 45

Codes, for focusing on text, 58-59

Collaborative learning, concept map for, 32-33, 117

Communication with parents, with textbook adaptation plan, 30

Compacting Contract, for compacting the curriculum, 34, 35; reproducible for, 119

Compacting Record, for compacting the curriculum, 34, 35; reproducible for, 121

Compacting the curriculum: reproducibles for, 118-21; for teaching material not yet mastered, 34-35

Comprehension. See Listening comprehension; Reading comprehension

Computation errors in math, reducing, 28, 60

Concentration, headphones improving, 65

Concept map: for activating prior knowledge about subject, 32-33; reproducible for, 117

Content Puzzles, for taking notes and remembering information, 68; reproducible for, 130

Copying errors in math, reducing, 62

Copying textbook material. See Photocopying textbook material

Craft sticks, for randomly grouping students, 15

Crossword puzzles, for introducing and reinforcing vocabulary, 80

D

Decimals, reinforcing, in random grouping activity, 14, 102-3

Differences between students, preventing stigma from, 29, 65

Differentiating textbooks: definition of, xi; as "part of good teaching," xii

Division problems, reducing errors in, 28

Drawing, for committing information to long-term memory, 85

During-reading strategies, xii; for focusing on text, 56, 58-59, 60, 61, 73, 126, 128; for improving comprehension, 63, 64; for improving concentration, 65; for Irlen Syndrome/Scotopic Sensitivity, 57; for math word problems, 74, 137; note taking, 66-67, 68, 69, 70, 130-36; purpose of, 55; for reading support, 71; for reducing copying errors in math, 62; for summarizing reading material, 72; for visualizing text, 75, 76

E

English Language Learner, online vocabulary help for, 41

Enlarging copies of textbook: for aiding visual difficulty with small print, 29; for making visual aids, 49

Equivalent Decimals, Percents, and Fractions: for forming random grouping, 14; reproducibles for, 102-3

Estimating math answers, 41; reproducible for, 124

Exit cards, for reinforcing learning, 91

Expository text: characteristics of, xi; illustrating, 63; improving understanding of, xii

Extension Activity Menu: for compacting the curriculum, 34, 35; reproducible for, 120

Eye-tracking difficulty, reading tool for, 56, 126

F

504 students, xi

Flash cards, talking, for learning vocabulary, 40

Focus Frame: for focusing on text, 60; reproducible for, 128

Focusing on text, during-reading strategies for, 56, 58-59, 60, 61, 73, 126, 128

Forms. See Reproducibles

Four Corners Voting, for expressing opinions, 94

Fox, Mem, 90

Fractions, reinforcing, in random grouping activity, 14, 102-3

G

Geography: attribute cards for, 18; pairing students in, 18

Graphic, for committing information to long-term memory, 85

Graphic organizers: concept map, 32-33, 117; Math Word Problem, 74, 137; note taking with, 69; reproducibles for, 130-35

Greet and Go, for predicting and setting purposes for reading, 46

Grouping arrangements, 13; randomly selected. See Random groupings

Groups of four, activities for forming, 16-17, 21-22, 104

Groups of three, activities for forming, 14, 20, 102-3, 112

Groups of two, activities for forming, 18, 19, 21-22, 105-10, 111

Guess the Word: for learning content-area vocabulary, 37; reproducible for, 123

Guided practice, for creating independent learners, xii

H

Headings and subheadings, rewriting, 26

Headphones, noise-suppressing, for improving concentration, 65

Highlighting marker, 54

Highlighting tape, 54

Highlighting text, for focusing attention on details, 54

History timelines, 73

Homework support, from letter-clues, 79

I

Illustrations, for improving reading comprehension, 63

Independent learners, creating, xii, 26

Index cards: for creating groups of four, 16, 17; for creating groups of three, 14; for exit cards, 91; for Greet and Go activity, 46; for pairing students, 18; for Power Thinking activity, 66; for textbook pictionary, 87; for Three Facts and a Fib activity, 88; vocabulary, 38

Information grid: for organizing, categorizing, and analyzing information, 81; reproducible for, 138

Inside/outside review circles, for responding to textbook questions, 78

Interview, three-step, for summarizing reading material, 72

Irlen Syndrome/Scotopic Sensitivity: colored overlays helping, 57; self-test for, 127

K

Keep-Your-Place reading tool, for focusing on text, 56; reproducible for, 126

Knowledge of subject, expanding, 100, 141; prior: activating, 31, 32-33, 43, 53; assessing, 34, 45; summarizing, 44

KWL (What I Know, What I Want to Know, and What I Learned): for activating prior knowledge of subject, 32-33; for compacting the curriculum, 34, 35; reproducibles for, 117, 118

L

Laminated chapter books, as textbook adaptation, 24

Language arts, pairing students in, 18

Large-print textbooks, for aiding visual difficulty, 29

Learning from textbook, difficulty with, 30, 114-16

Learning objectives, assessing, for compacting the curriculum, 34

Letter-clues, for homework questions, 79

Leveling questions, for finding literal vs. inferential answers, 82-83

Listening comprehension, recorded textbooks improving, 64

List-Group-Label, for preparing to read textbook, 42

Long-term memory, committing information to, 85

M

Mailing labels, for substituting headings and subheadings, 26

Marker, highlighting, 54

Match-the-Meaning Card Game: reproducible for, 139; for reviewing vocabulary, 95

Math: estimating answers in, 51, 124; homework support in, 79; illustrating word problems in, 63; leveling questions in, 83; pairing students in, 18; reducing computation errors in, 28, 60; reducing copying errors in, 62; reinforcing decimals, percents, and fractions in, 14, 102-3; reviewing concept or skill in, 93; Word Problem Graphic Organizer for,

74, 137; word problem visuals for, 50

Math Answer Estimates, reproducible for, 124

Math equivalent cards: in grouping activity, 14; reproducible, 102-3

Math games, grouping students into threes for, 20, 112

Memory, long-term, committing information to, 85

Memory boxes, for reviewing text, 90

Merriam-Webster web site, for vocabulary help, 41

Mind maps, for nonlinguistic representation of text, 75

Mixed operations, in math problems, 28

Modeling, think-aloud: for comprehension of textbook, 48; for R.E.A.D.S. strategy, 97

Motivation to read textbook: Anticipation Guide for, 43; as before-reading strategy, 31; concept map for, 32-33, 117

Multiplication problems, reducing errors in, 28

Music, pairing students in, 18

N

Narrative text, characteristics of, xi

Noise-suppressing headphones, for improving concentration, 65

Note taking: with graphic organizers, 69, 131-35; Power Thinking for, 66-67; with Textbook Talk-back Notes, 70, 136

O

Online vocabulary help, 41

Onomatopoeia, as visualization activity, 76

Opinions, expressing, with Four Corners Voting, 94

Organizational strategies: cloze activity, 45; for reducing computation errors in math problems, 28

Organizers, graphic. See Graphic organizers

Organizing, categorizing, and analyzing: as after-reading strategy, 81; reproducible for, 138

Overhead transparencies: for interpreting and understanding data, 49; for showing student illustrations of text, 63; for Textbook Look-back activity, 98

P

Pair Cards, for states and capitals, reproducible for, 105-10

Pairing activities, for grouping students, 18, 19, 21-22, 105-10, 111

Percents, reinforcing, in random grouping activity, 14, 102-3

Permission from publisher: to enlarge copies of textbook,

29; to photocopy textbooks, 25, 49; to record textbooks, 64; reproducible form for, 113

Personal Learning Timelines, for focusing on information, 73

Photocopying textbook material: for enlarging textbooks, 29; for making chapter books, 25; for making visual aids, 49; obtaining publishers' permission for, 25, 49, 113

Physical education, pairing students in, 18

Pictionary, textbook, for vocabulary help, 87

Pieces of Eight, for reviewing concept or skill, 93

Poetry, pairing students in, 18

Pointer/Signal Words: for pre-reading textbook chapter, 52, 69; reproducible for, 125

Popsicle sticks, for randomly grouping students, 15

Post-it notes: for answering end-of-chapter questions, 92; for focusing on text, 58-59

Potluck Reading, for summarizing textbook information, 84

Power Thinking, for note-taking, 66-67

Predictions about reading: cloze activity for, 45; Greet and Go for, 46; Word Toss for, 47

Prefixes and Suffixes, reproducible for, 123

Pre-reading textbook chapter, 52; reproducible for, 125

Pretest, for assessing prior knowledge of subject, 34

Primary sources, reproducible for, 141

Processing information: R.A.F.T. activity for, 86; with Three Facts and a Fib, 88

Pros, Cons, and What I Wonder, for setting purpose for reading, 36; reproducible for, 122

Purposes for reading, setting: as before-reading strategy, 31, 36, 43, 45, 46, 47, 122; as during-reading strategy, 58

Puzzles: content, for taking notes and remembering information, 68, 130; crossword, for introducing and reinforcing vocabulary, 80

Q

Questions: answering, with taped responses, 89; end-of-chapter, answering, 92, 98; homework, letter-clues for, 79; leveling, for finding literal vs. inferential answers, 82-83; review circles for responding to, 78; short-answer, improving responses to, 96-97

R

R.A.F.T., for processing information, 86

Random groupings, xii, 13

activities for: attribute cards, 16-17, 104; card games, 21-22; Circle of Three, 20, 112; Clock Partners, 19, 111; Equivalent Decimals, Percents, and Fractions, 14, 102-3; pairing up for learning, 18, 105-10; Popsicle sticks, 15

Reading, pairing students in, 18

Reading comprehension: taped vocabulary words for, 39; think-aloud modeling for, 48; visualization improving, 63

Reading difficulty: eliminating unnecessary information for, 27; improving listening comprehension in, 64; from Irlen Syndrome/Scotopic Sensitivity, 57, 127

Reading support, with Read-Pair-Share, 71

Reading tool: for focusing on small amount of text, 56; reproducible for, 126

Read-Pair-Share: for Post-it note discussion, 59; for reading support, 71

R.E.A.D.S. (RE-state, Answer, Details, State again), for responding to short-answer questions, 96-97

Recording textbook material, 64; permission form for, 113

Reproducibles: Active Bookmarks, 129; Clock Partners, 111; Compacting Contract, 119; Compacting Record, 121; Concept Map, 117; Content Puzzle, 130; Extension Activity Menu, 120; Finding the Evidence Through Primary Sources, 141; Focus Frame, 128; graphic organizers, 130-35; information grid, 138; Keep-Your-Place Reading Tool Pattern, 126; Match-the-Meaning Cards, 139; Math Answer Estimates, 124; Math Equivalents Cards, 102-3; Math Word Problem Graphic Organizer, 137; Pair Cards for states and capitals, 105-10; Pointer/Signal Words, 125; Prefixes and Suffixes, 123; Pros, Cons, and What I Wonder chart, 122; request form for permission to copy or record, 113; Self-test for Irlen Syndrome/Scotopic Sensitivity, 127; Textbook Adaptation Plan, 114-16; Textbook Look-back, 140; Textbook Talk-back Notes, 136; What I Know...What I Wonder...What I Learned, 118

Review circles, inside/outside, for responding to textbook questions, 78

Reviewing text: with Pieces of Eight, 93; with souvenir or memory boxes, 90; with Three Facts and a Fib, 88

R.S.V.P. (Read-Summarize-Verify-Prediction Corrections), 53

S

Science: attribute cards for, 18; illustrating procedures

in, 63; pairing students in, 18; reviewing concept or skill in, 93; timelines in, 73

Selecting textbooks, guidelines for, 23

Singapore Math textbooks, 50

Small-print textbooks, visual difficulty with, 29

Souvenirs, for reviewing text, 90

Special needs students, xi

States and capitals Pair Cards, reproducibles for, 105-10

Struggling students, xi, xii; answering end-of-chapter questions, 92; collaborative learning for, 32; eliminating unnecessary information for, 27; recorded textbooks for, 64

Subheadings, headings and, rewriting, 26

Subtraction problems, reducing errors in, 28

Summarizing knowledge of subject, with timed responses, 44

Summarizing textbook information: with exit cards, 91; with Potluck Reading, 84; with Three-Step Interview, 72; in writing, 99

T

Talk-back Notes, Textbook: for note taking, 70, 136; reproducible for, 136

Talking flash cards, for learning vocabulary, 40

Tape: highlighting, 54; for substituting headings and subheadings, 26

Taped responses, as alternative to written answers, 89

Taped vocabulary words, 39

Textbook adaptation plan: for reducing learning difficulty, 30; reproducible for, 114-16

Textbook Look-back, 26; for answering end-of-chapter questions, 98; reproducible for, 140

Textbook pictionary, for vocabulary help, 87

Textbook Talk-back Notes: for note taking, 70; reproducible for, 136

Textbooks: adapting. See Adapting textbooks, strategies for differentiating: definition of, xi; as "part of good teaching," xii; difficulty learning from, 30, 114-16; drawbacks of, xi; guidelines for selecting, 23; math, reducing computation errors in, 28; overwhelming size of, 24-25; recorded, for improving listening comprehension, 64; requirements for comprehending, 31; rewriting headings and subheadings of, 26; unnecessary

information in, 27; visual difficulty with, 29

Think-aloud modeling: for comprehension of textbook, 48; for R.E.A.D.S. strategy, 97

Three Facts and a Fib, for reviewing text, 88

Three-Step Interview: grouping students into threes for, 20, 112; for summarizing reading material, 72

Timed responses, for summarizing knowledge, 44

Timelines, Personal Learning, for focusing on information, 73

U

Unnecessary text, eliminating, 27

V

Venn Diagram graphic organizer, for note taking, 69, 131

Visual aids: for interpreting and understanding data, 49; for math word problems, 50

Visual difficulty with small print, 29

Visualization: for improving reading comprehension, 63; mind maps for, 75; onomatopoeia for, 76

Vocabulary: before-reading strategies for introducing, 31, 37-42, 123; crossword puzzles for introducing and reinforcing, 80; Match-the-Meaning Card Game for reviewing, 95, 139; textbook pictionary for reviewing, 87

Vocabulary help, online, 41

Vocabulary index cards, 38

Vocabulary words, taped, 39

W

What I Know...What I Wonder...What I Learned: for compacting the curriculum, 34, 35; reproducible for, 118

Wilfrid Gordon McDonald Partridge, 90

Word Toss, for predicting and setting purposes for reading, 47

Writing: in R.A.F.T. activity, 86; of summaries, 99